ZODIAC SIGN ADULT COLORING BOOK

Just for Virgo

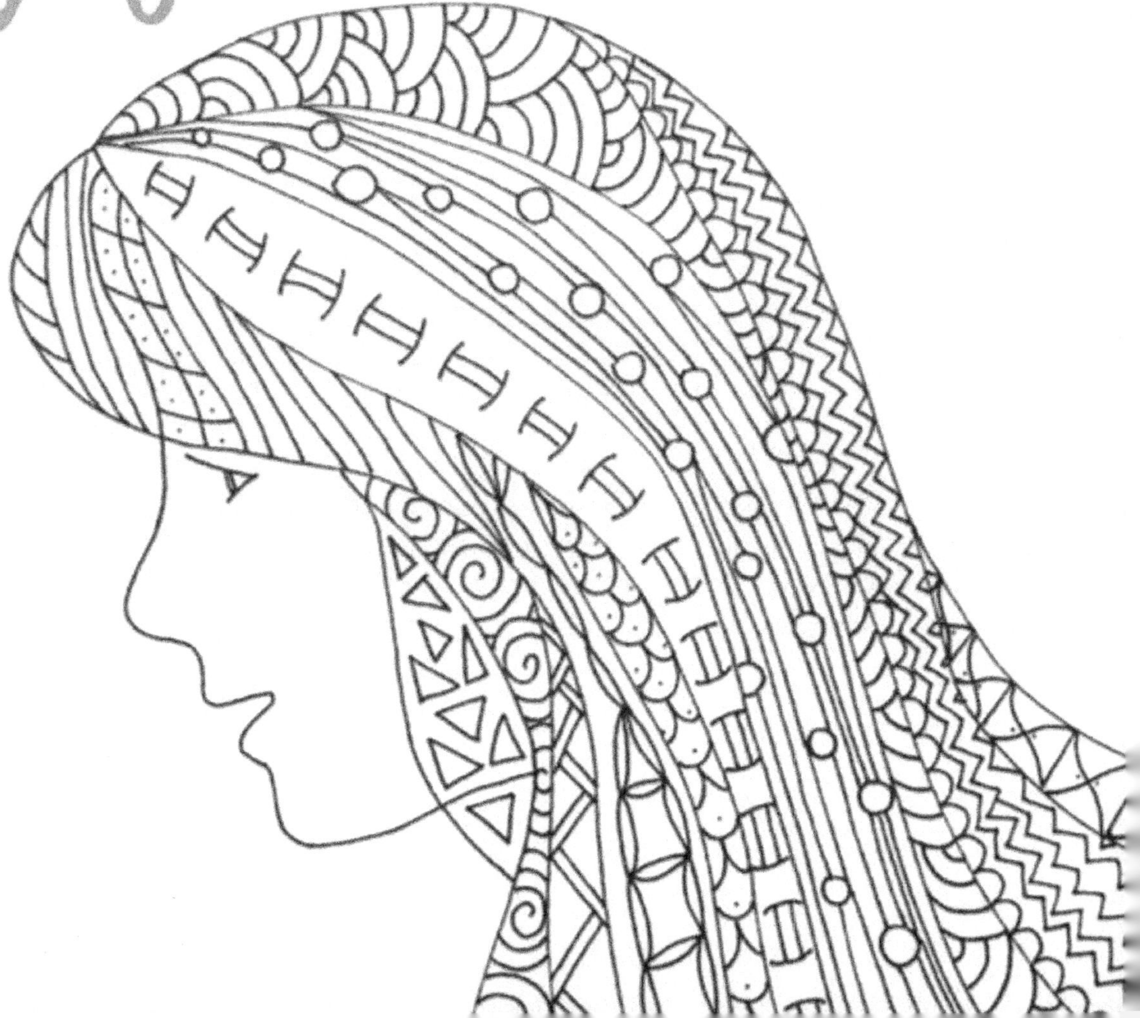

40 one-sided
coloring pages

Parker Street Books is an independent publisher of high quality adult coloring books, journals, and notebooks. Enjoy our exclusive designs, and personalize them to be uniquely yours. Relieve stress and refocus with mindful coloring. Parker Street books are fun, affordable, and found on Amazon. Thanks for being a fan!

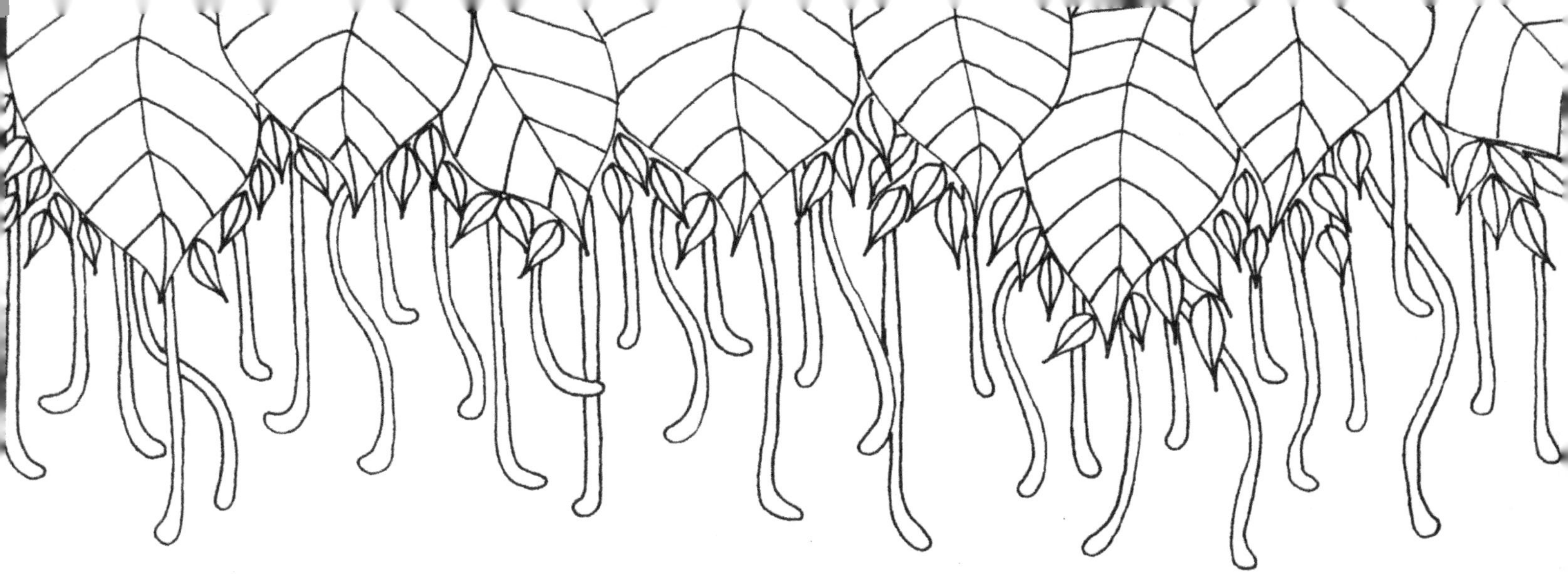

Virgo: The Virgin

If you're a Virgo, you're an achiever! You are a creative and lovely spirit who appreciates refinement and order. Precise, reliable, and caring—that's you. Your charm, intelligence, and meticulousness come from your planet ruler, Mercury. Your element, the Earth, suffuses you with kindness, reliability, and patience.

Virgo, you are prone to being a perfectionist, over thinker, and worrier which can squelch your naturally energetic and practical nature. Take some me-time to focus and unwind with meditative coloring. Virgo, savor this book full of designs geared towards your own personal signs and symbols.

Known for your compassion and service you may want to share your coloring pages, printed on only one side for easy removal. You love methodical exactness, Virgo, and mindful coloring allows you to create precise color combinations to your heart's content. Action oriented Virgo, get started and enjoy!

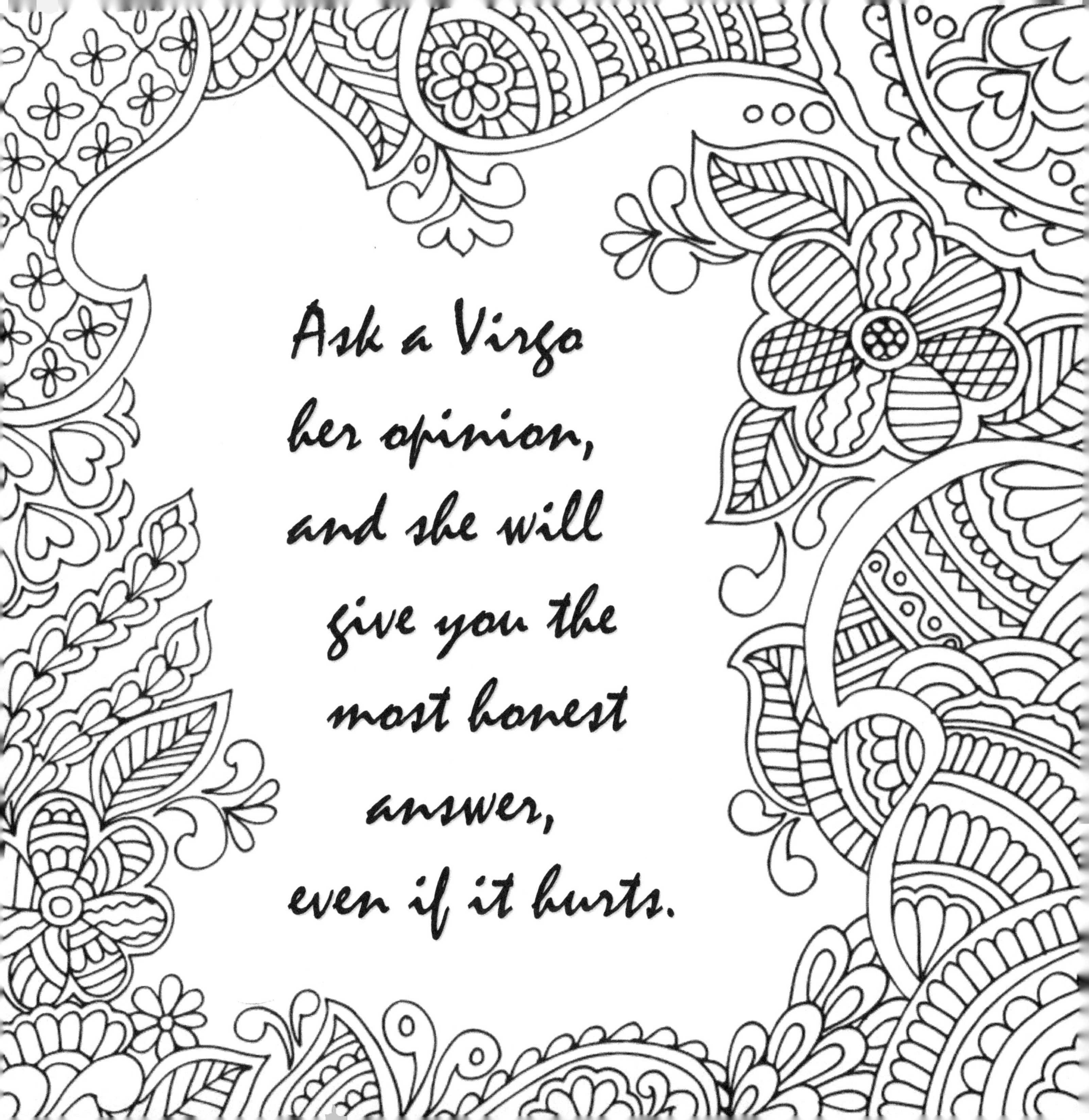
Ask a Virgo
her opinion,
and she will
give you the
most honest
answer,
even if it hurts.

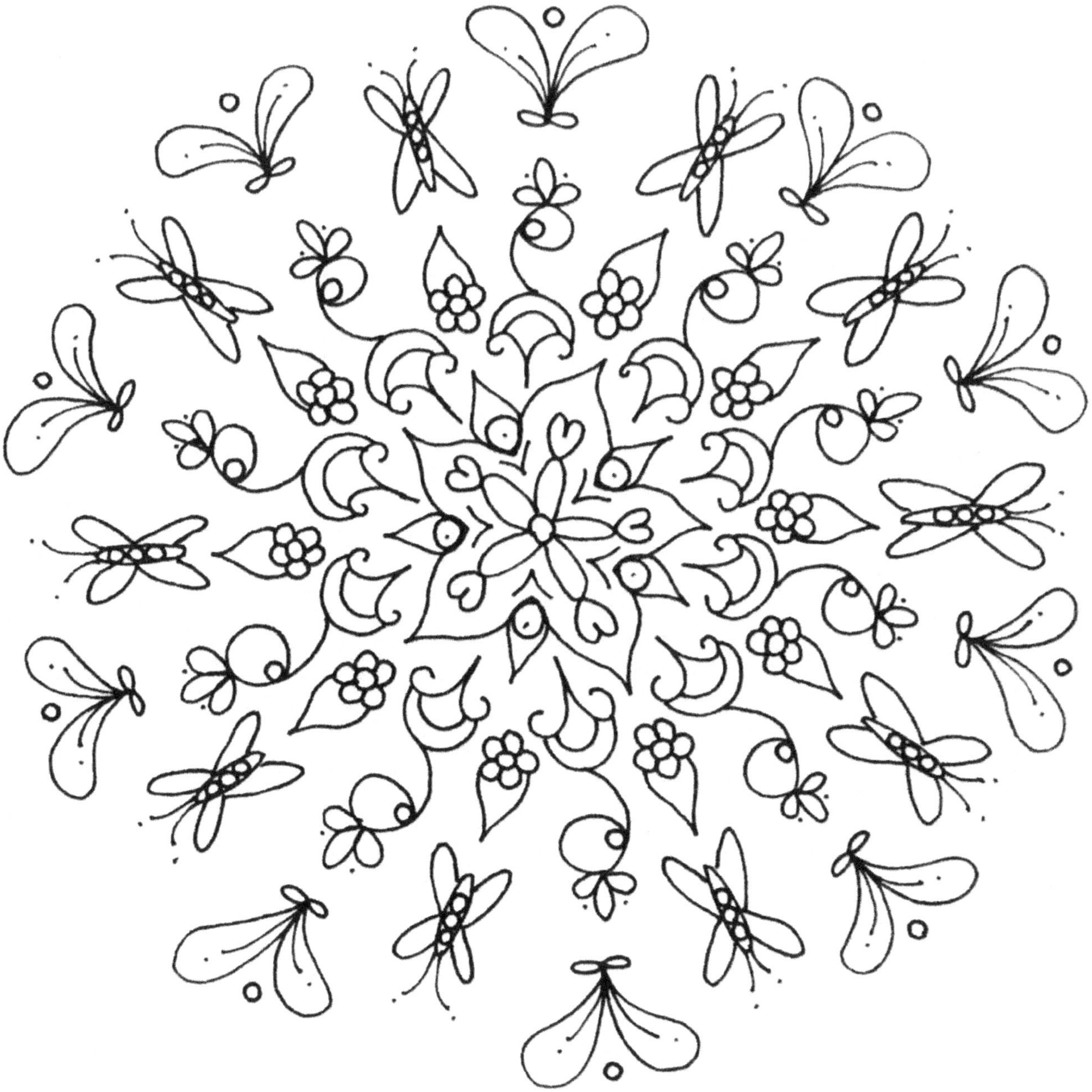

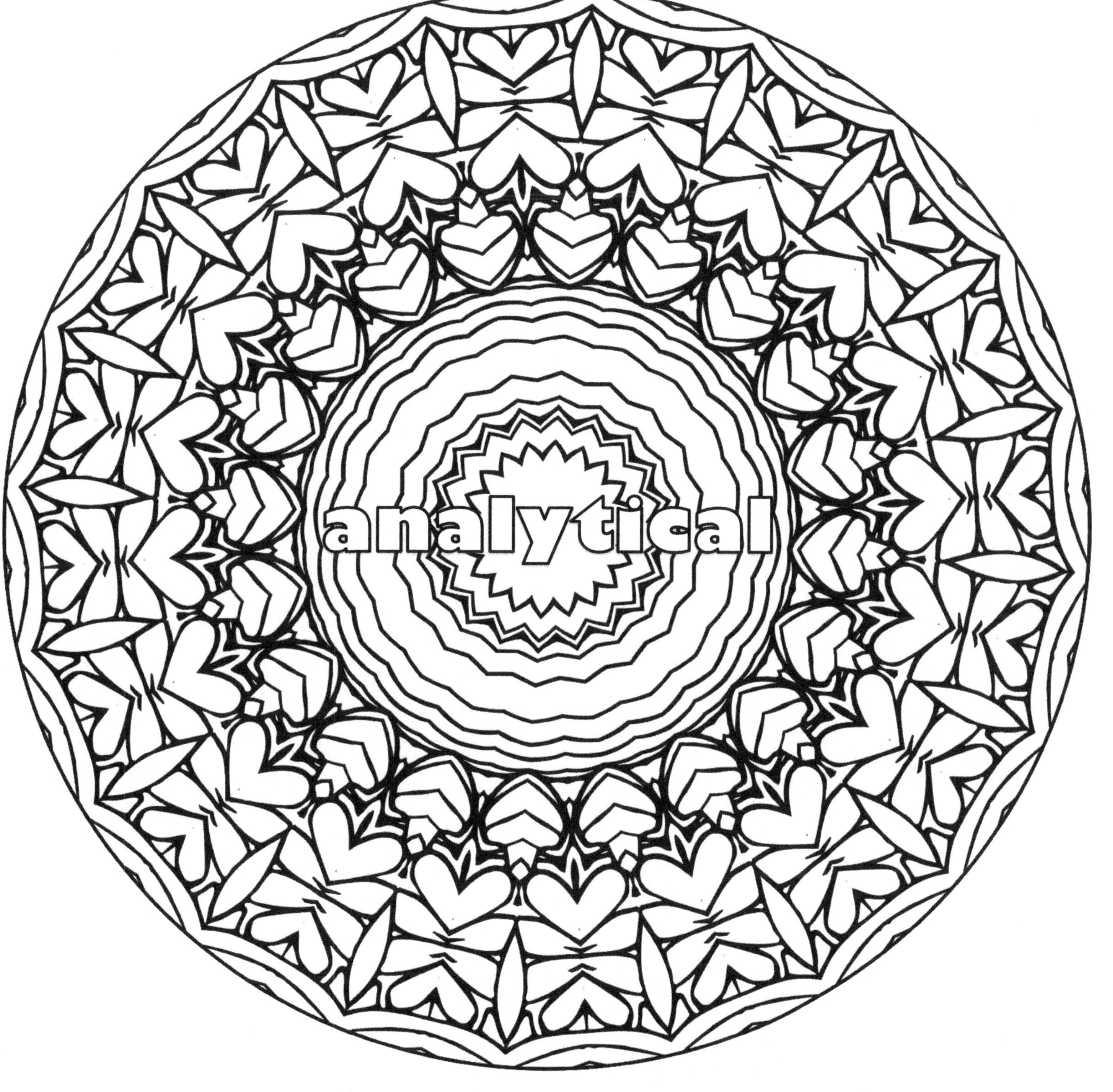
analytical

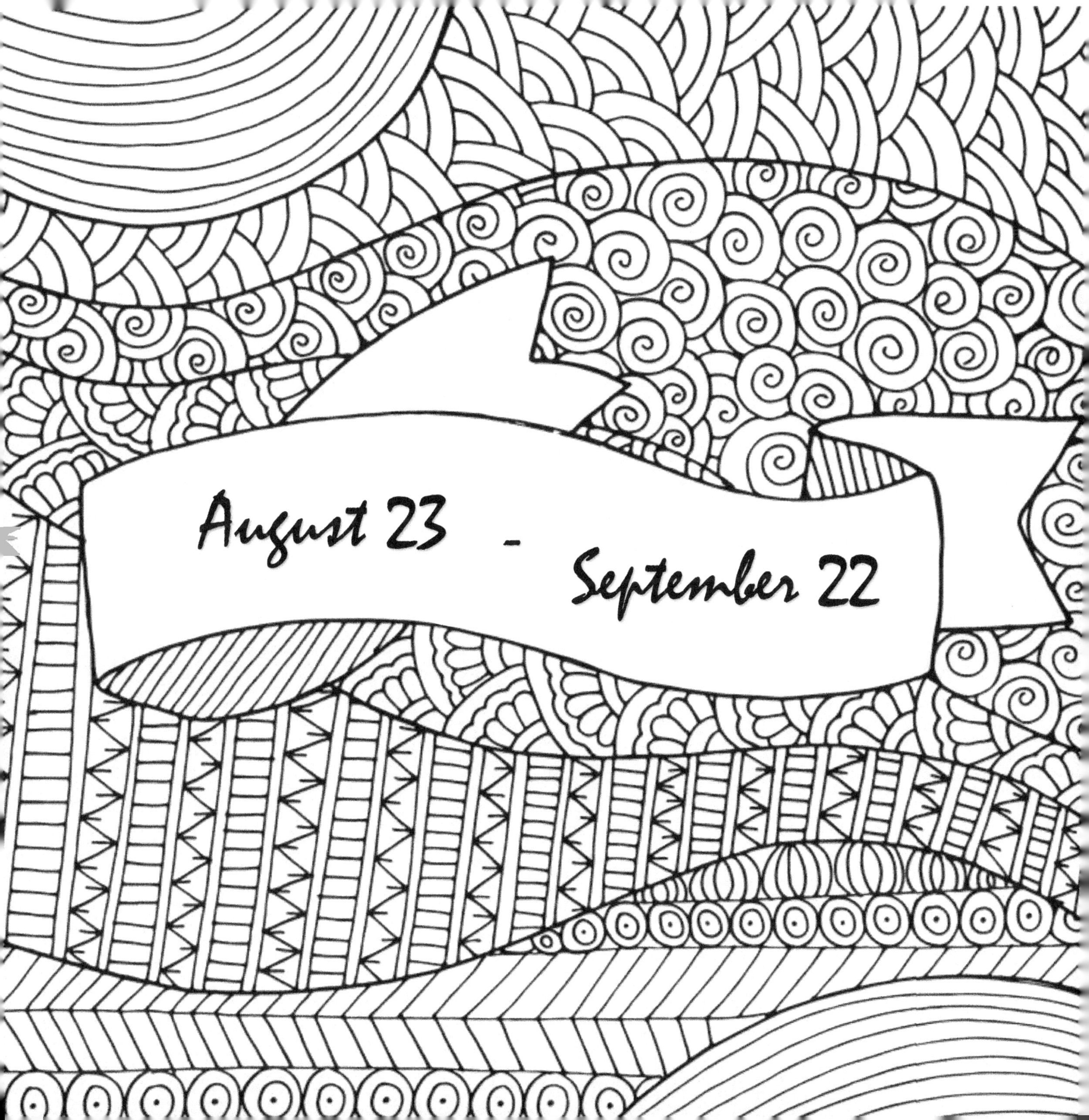
August 23 - September 22

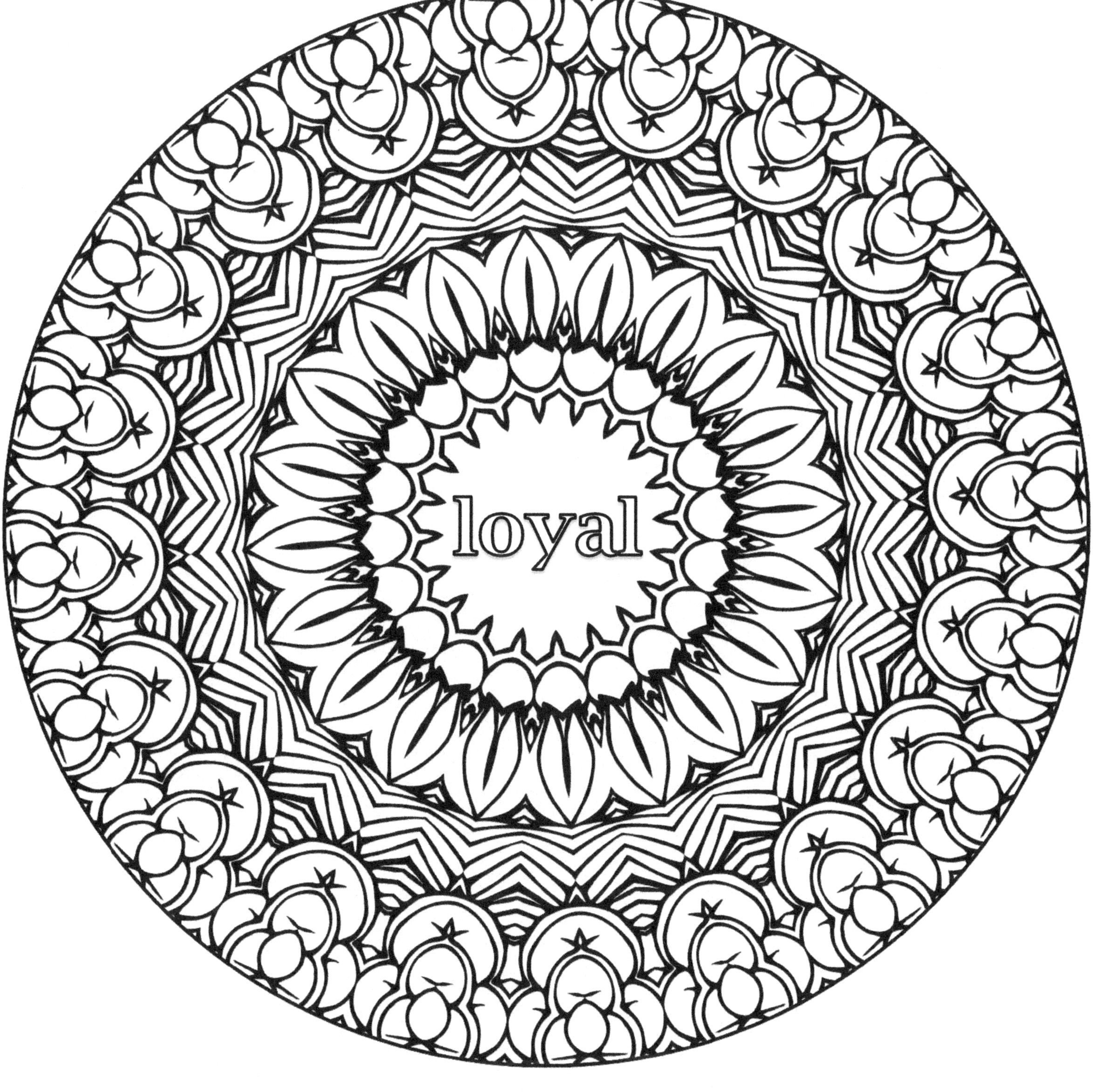
loyal

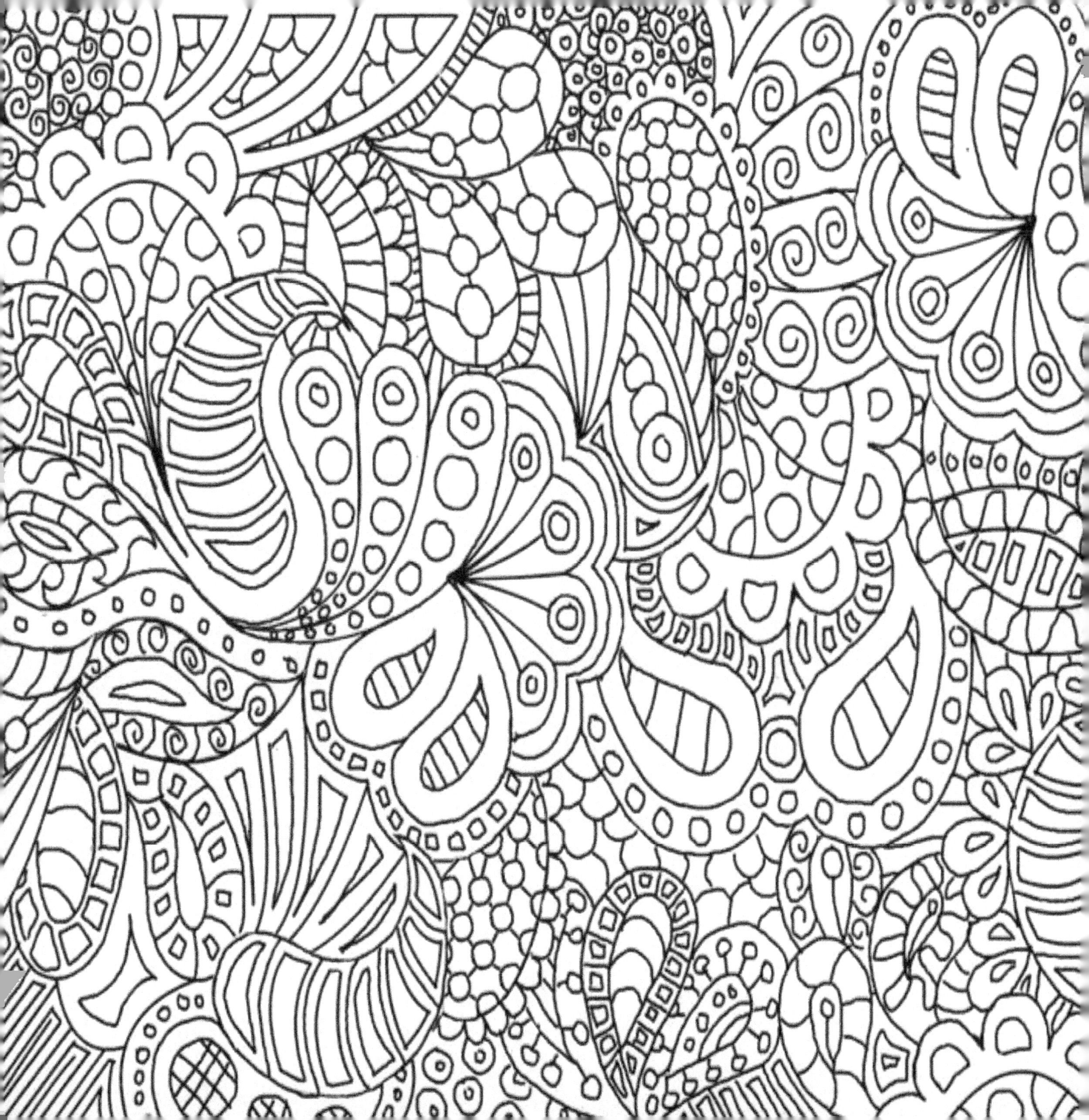

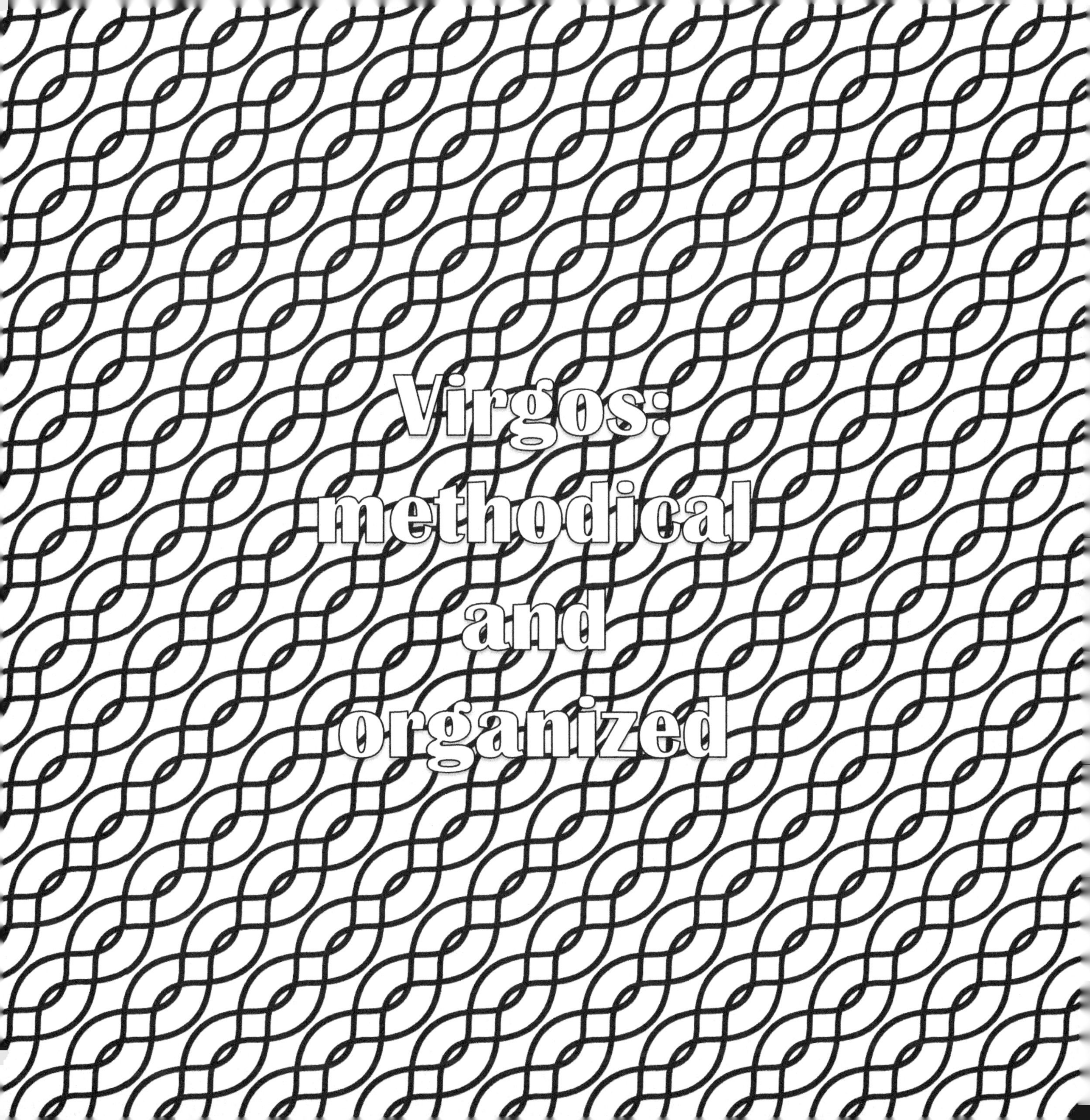
Virgos:
methodical
and
organized

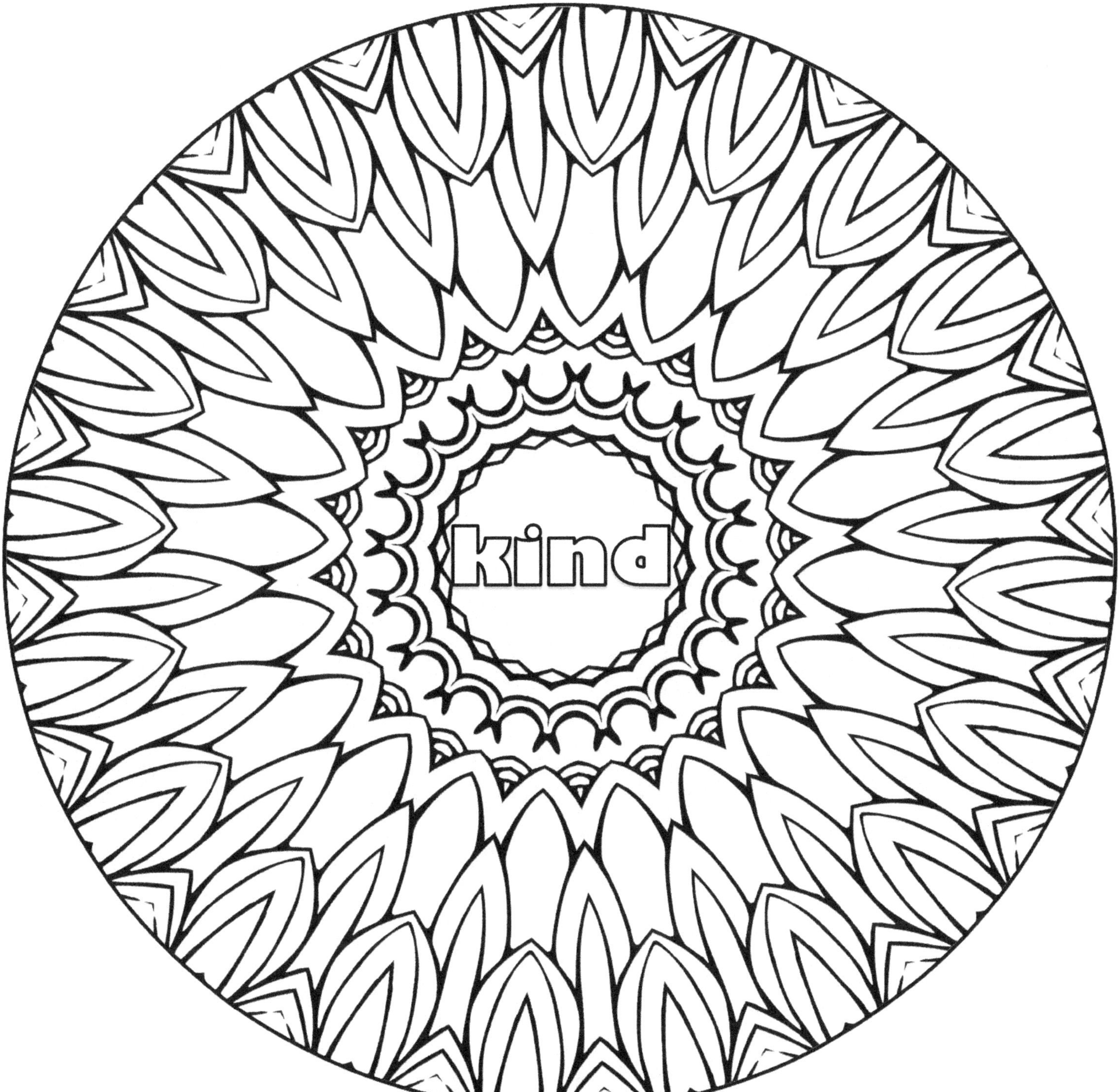
kind

Virgo:
Seeking Goodness In Humankind

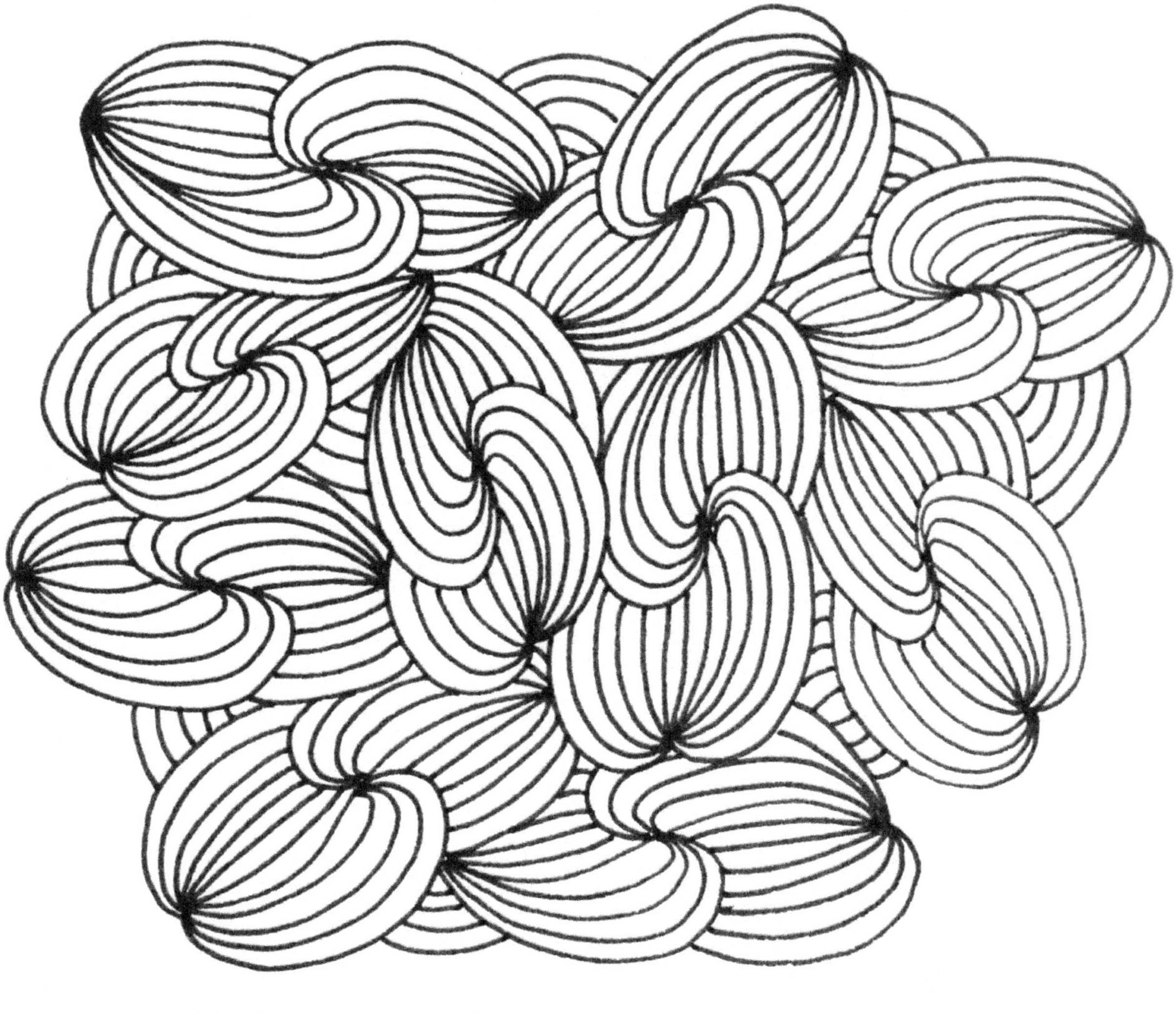

Hard-
working

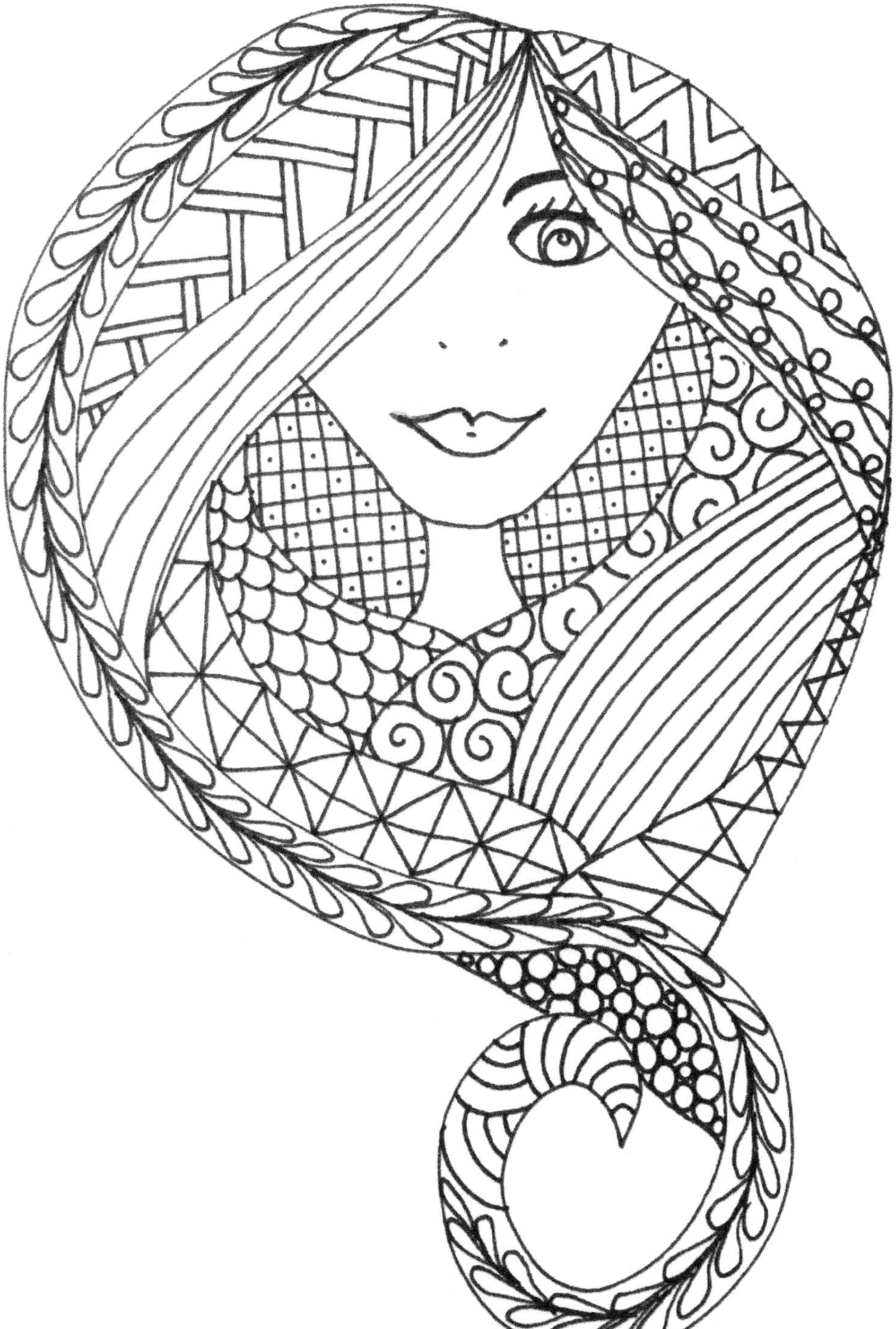

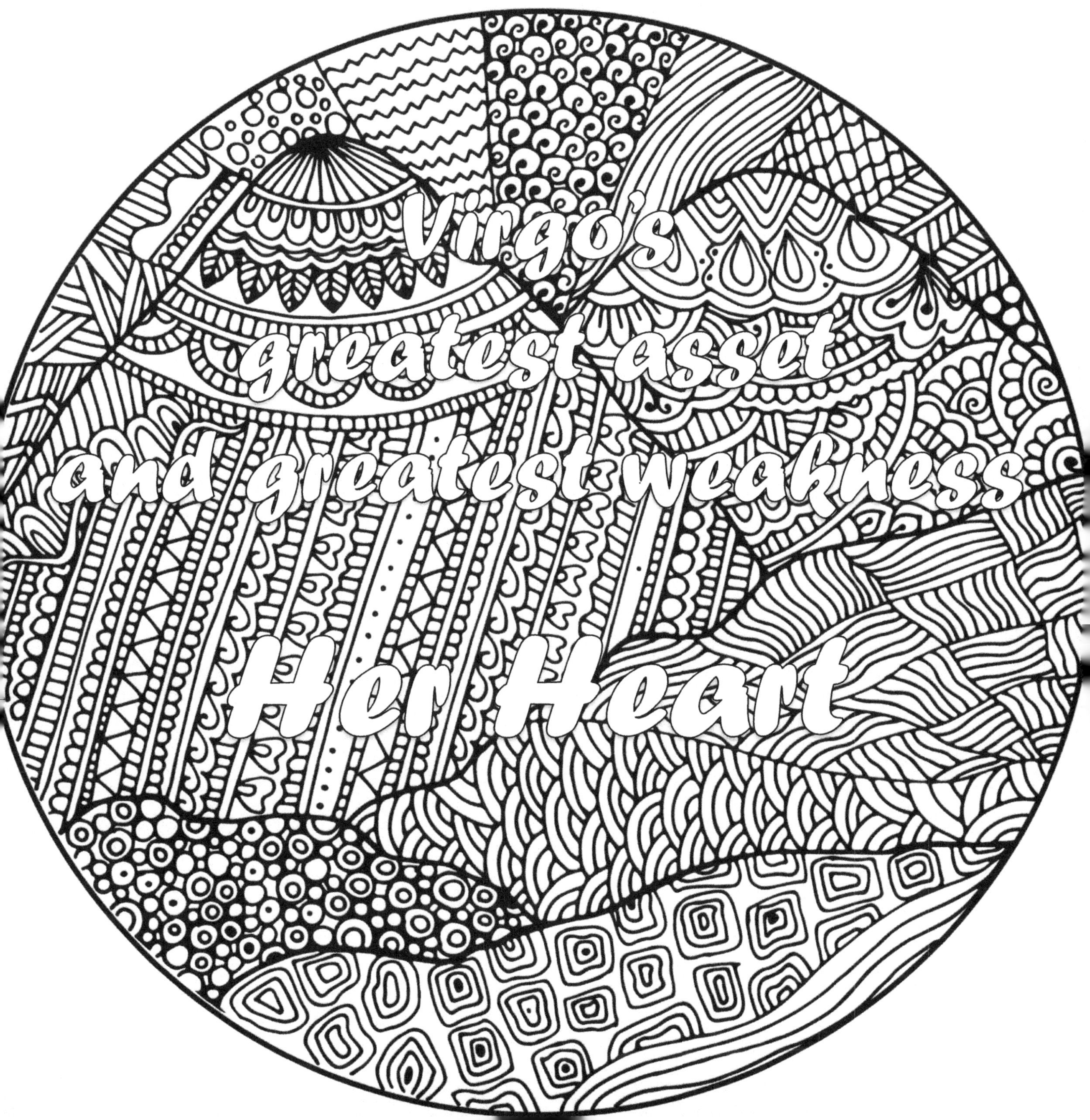
Virgo's
greatest asset
and greatest weakness
Her Heart

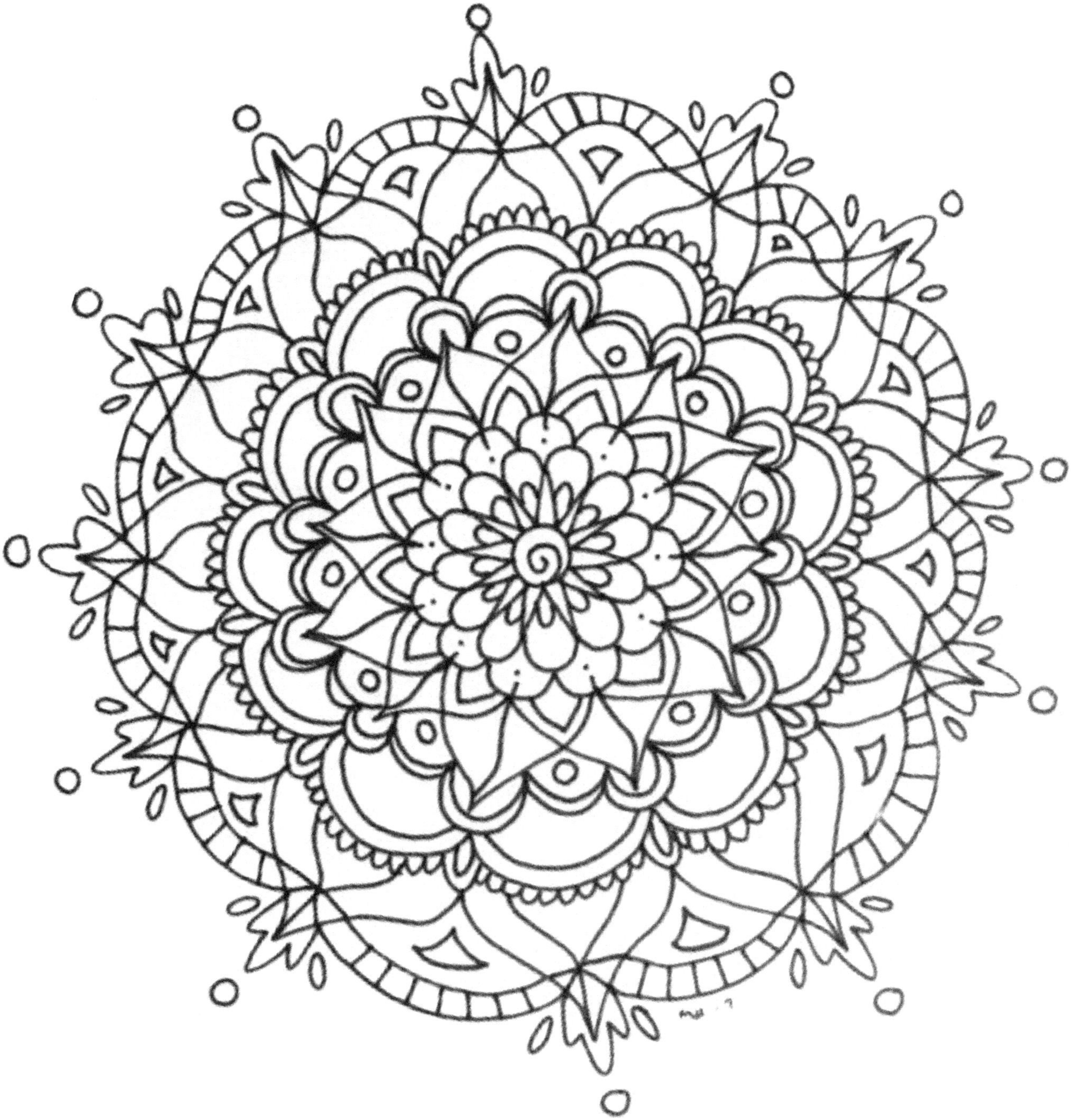

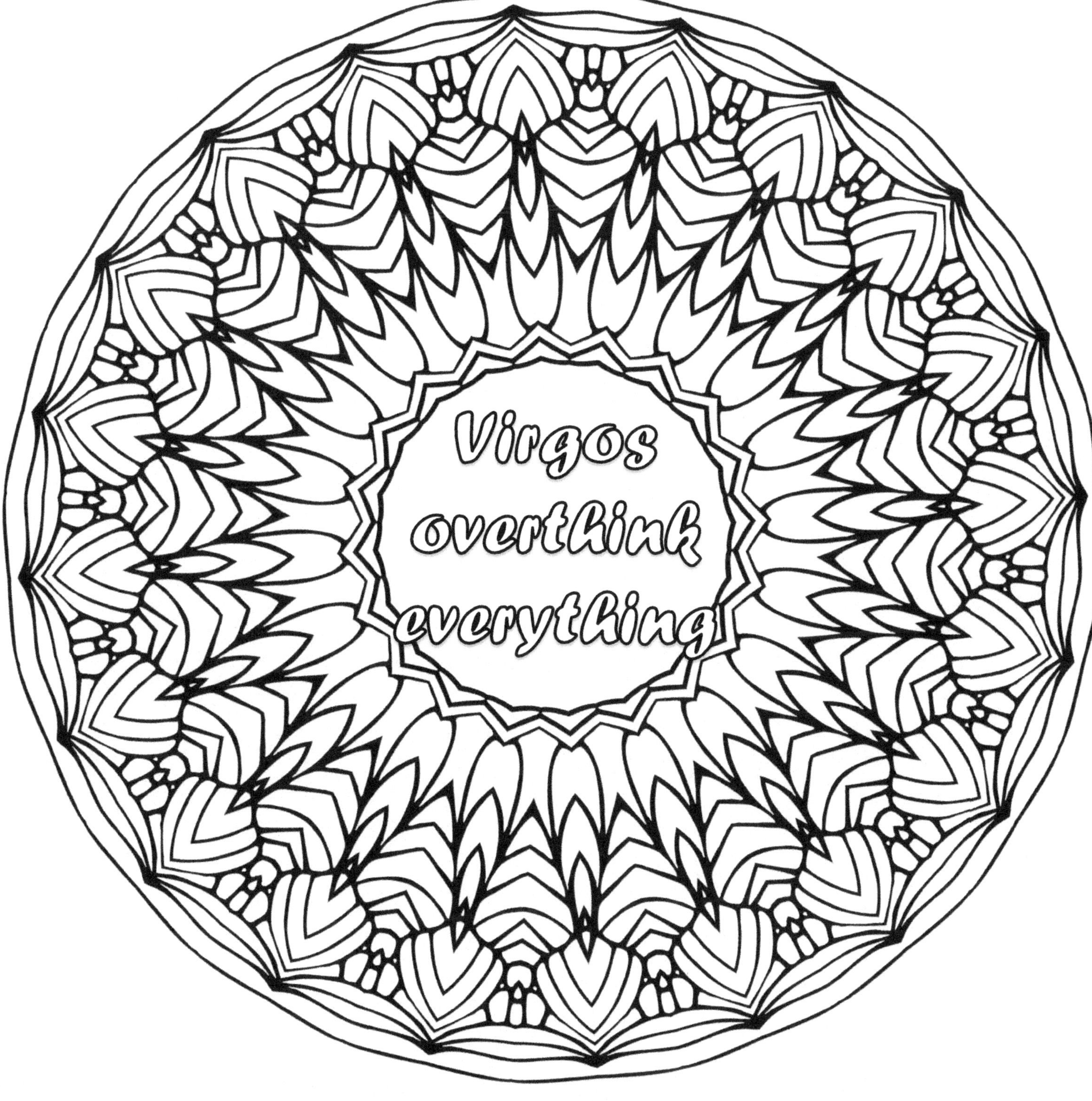
Virgos
overthink
everything

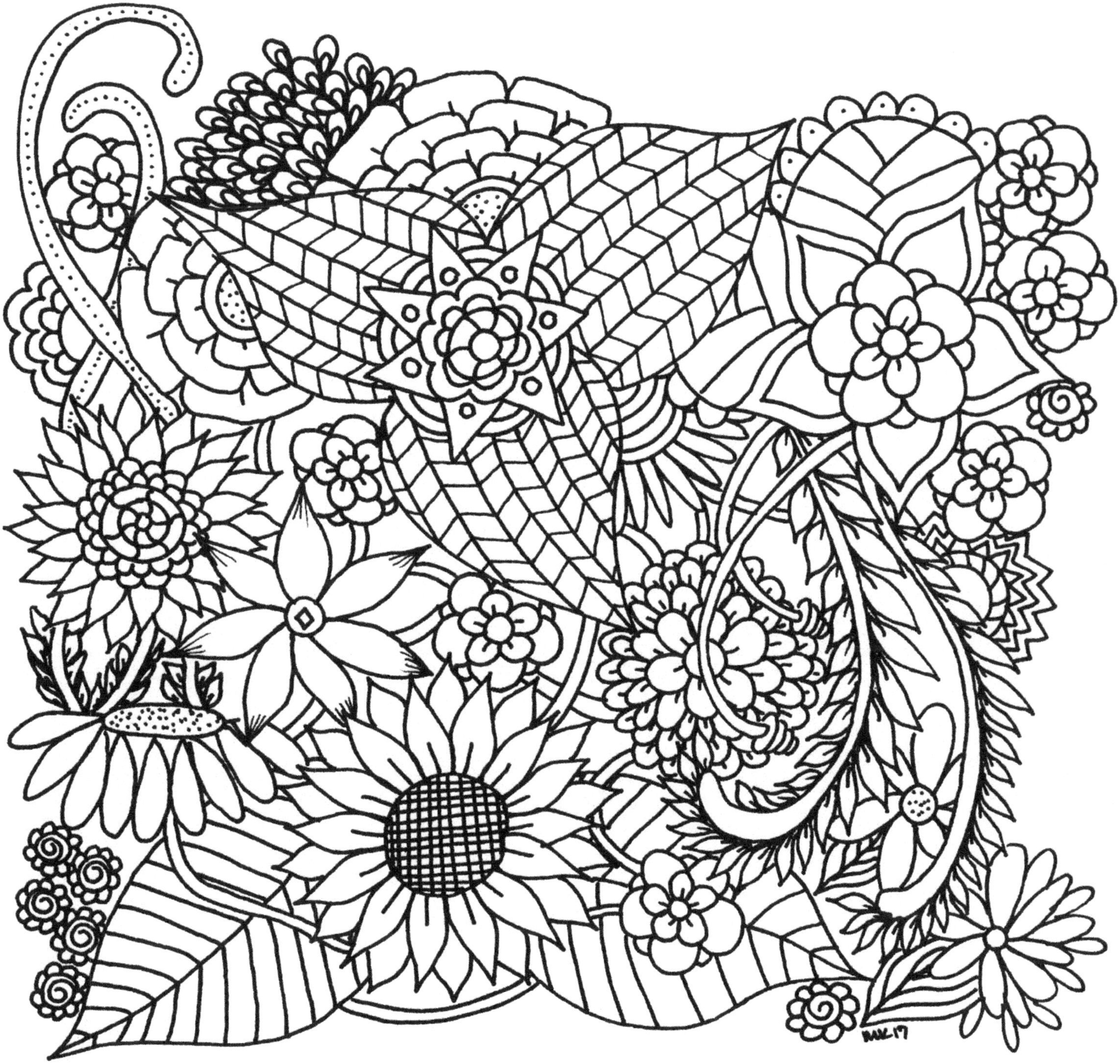

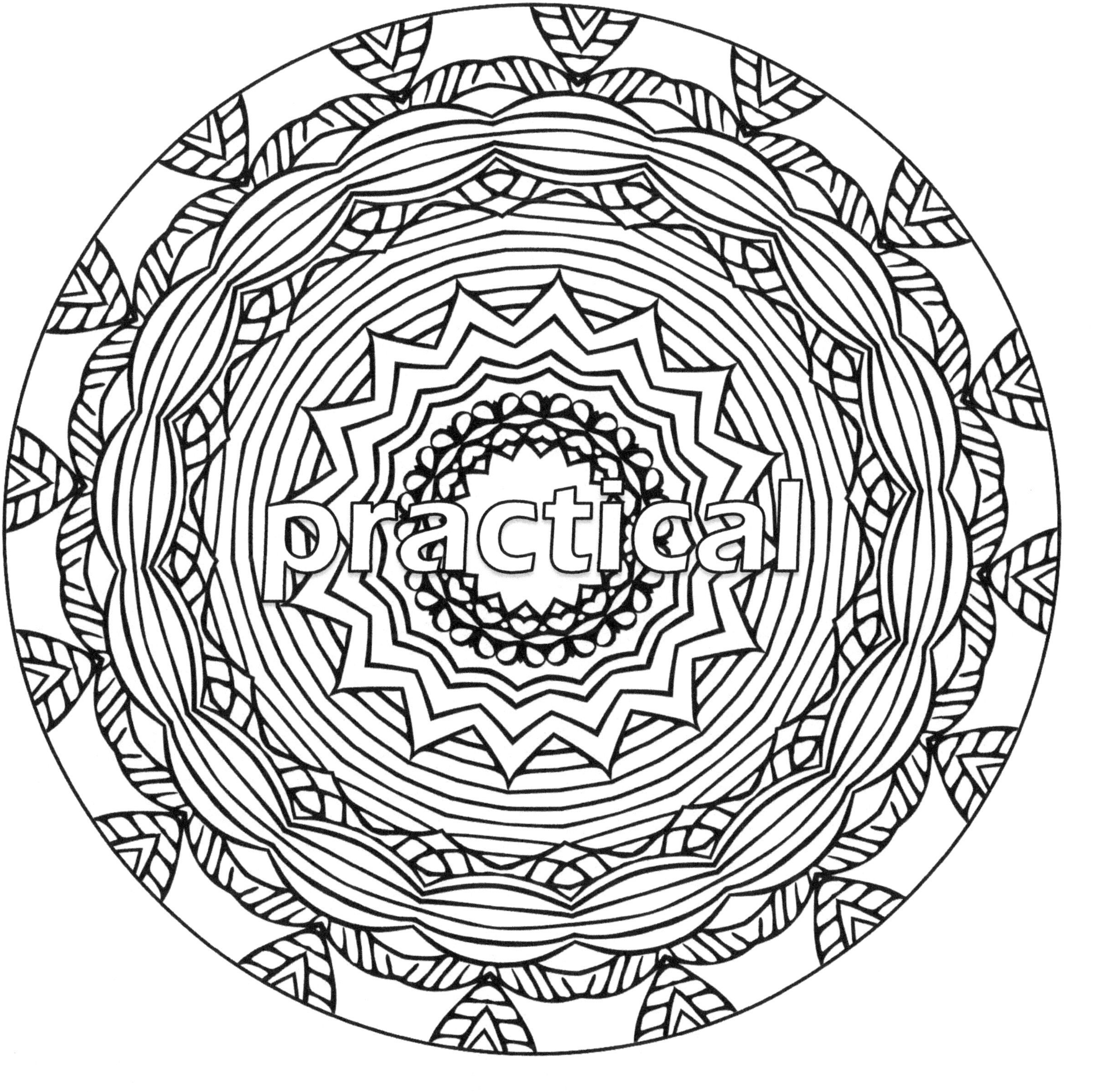
practical

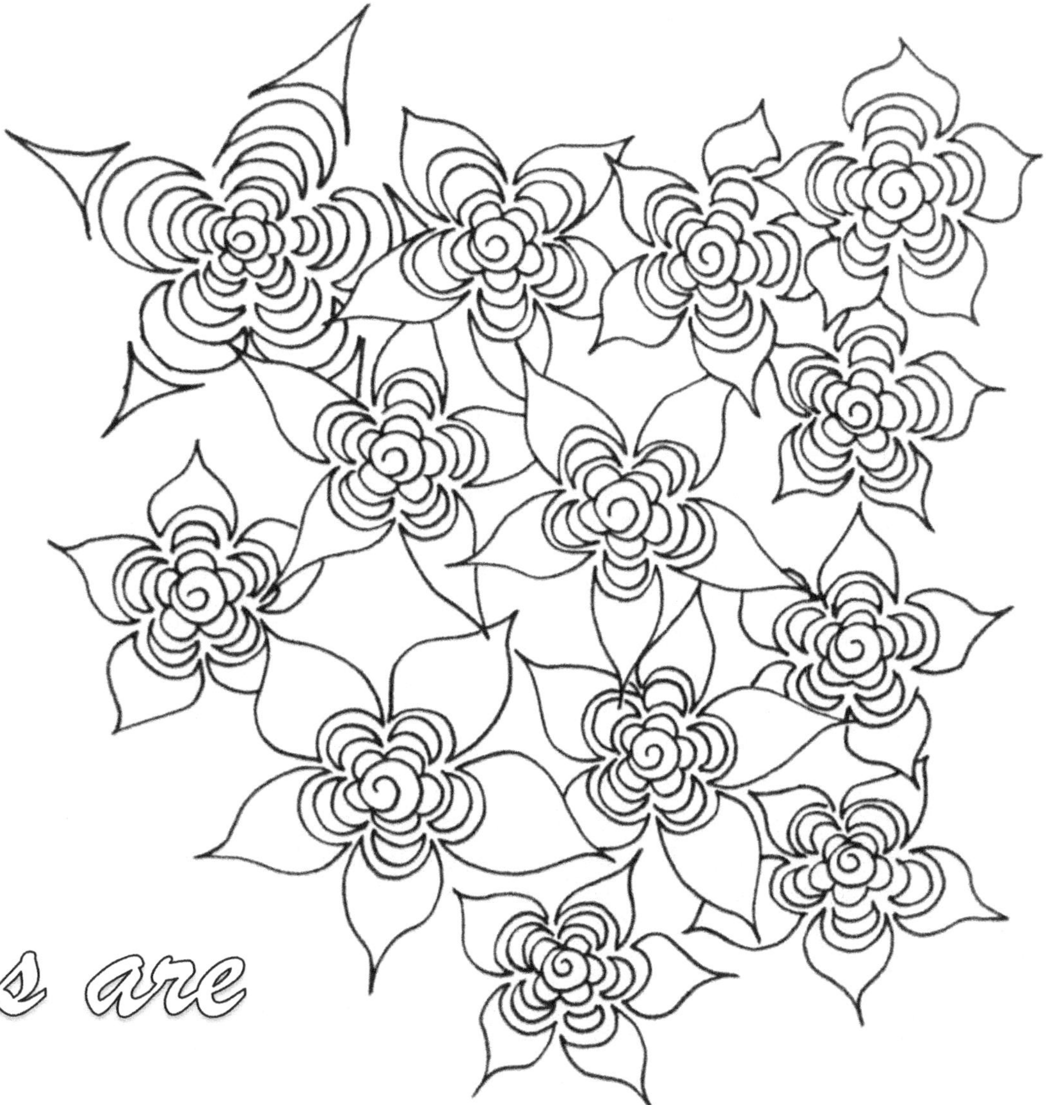

Virgos are dedicated friends.

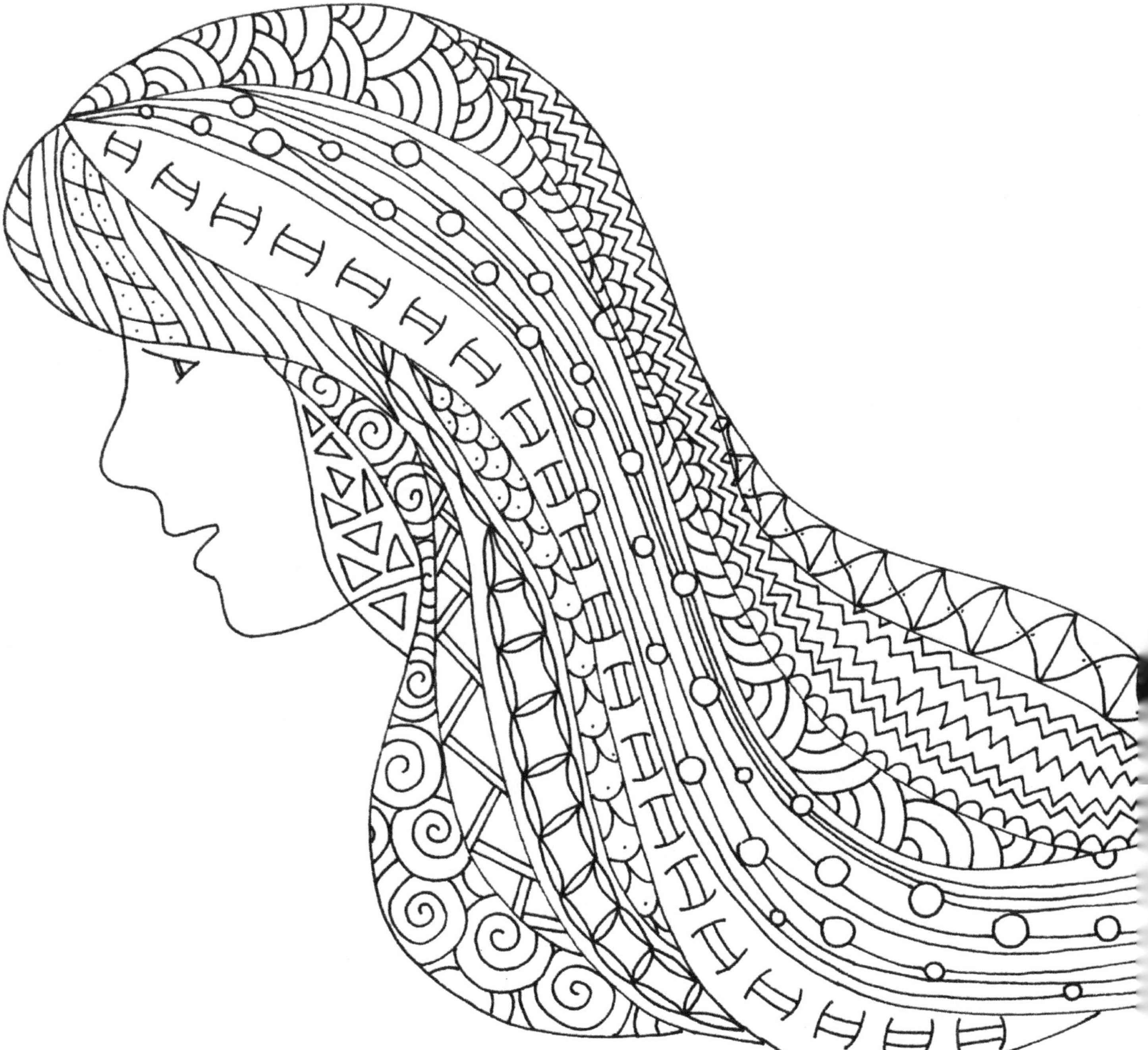

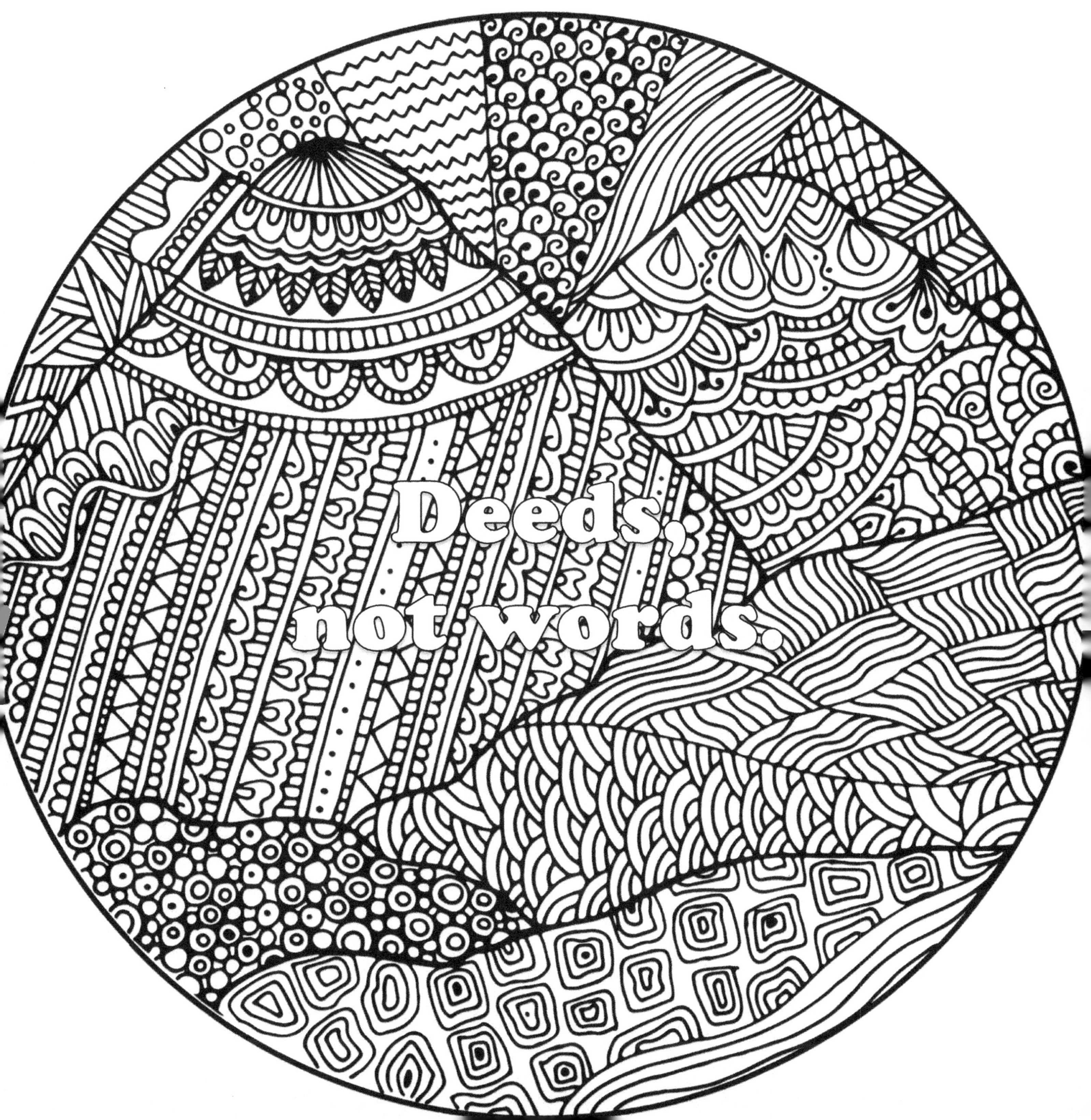
Deeds,
not words.

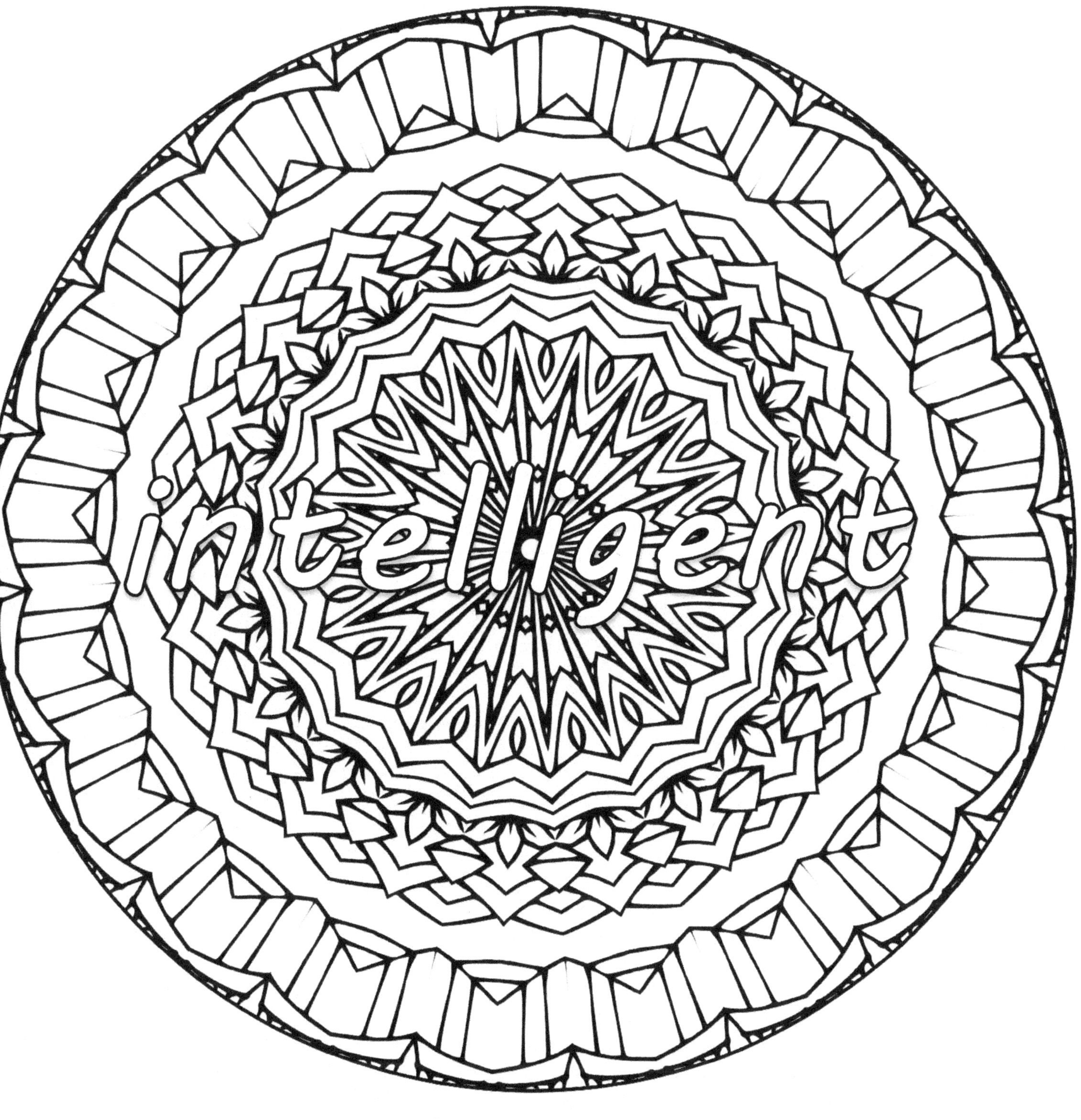
intelligent

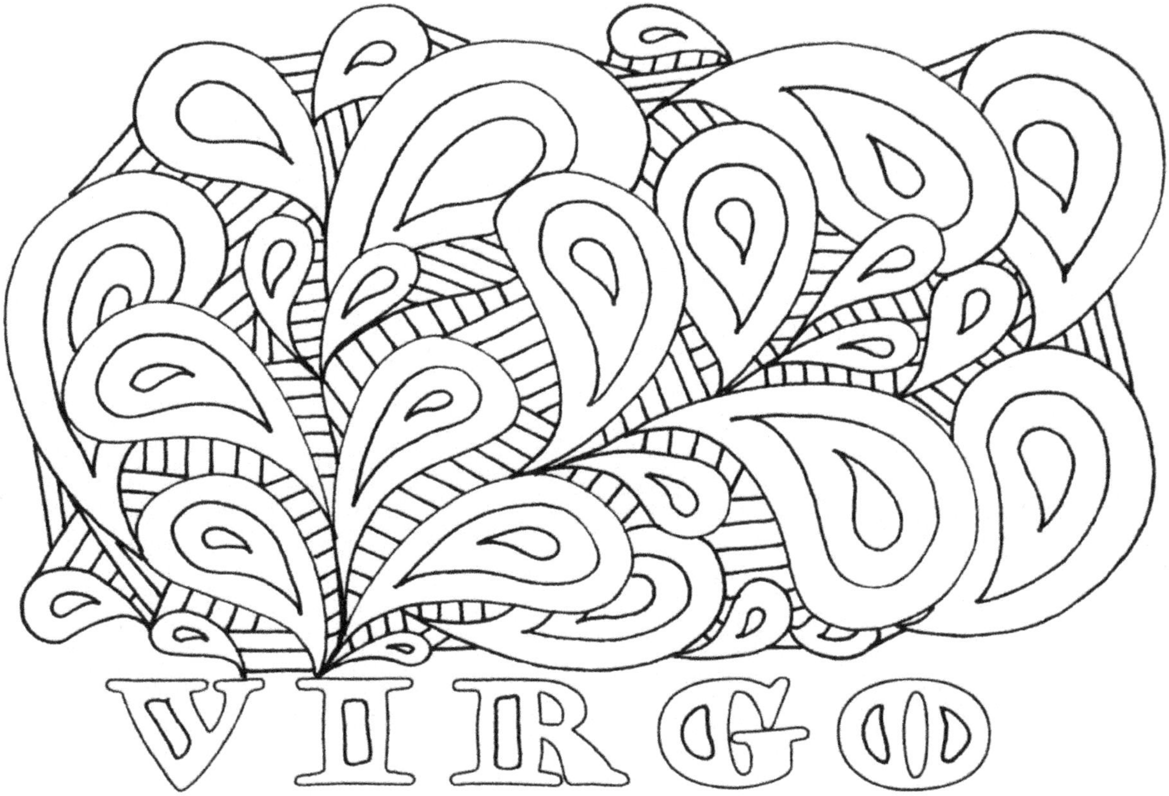
VIRGO

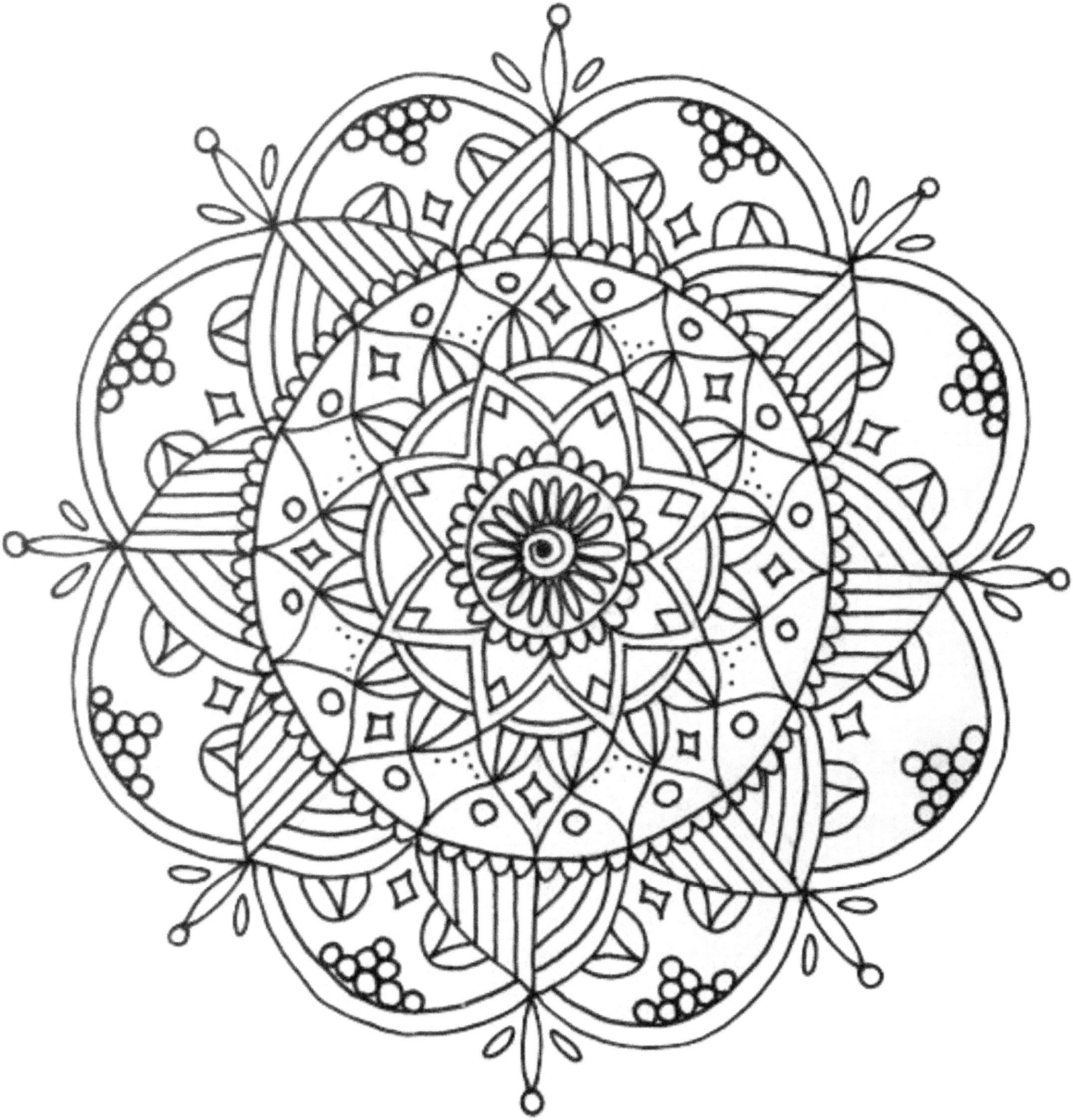

VIRGOS
PAY ATTENTION
TO DETAIL

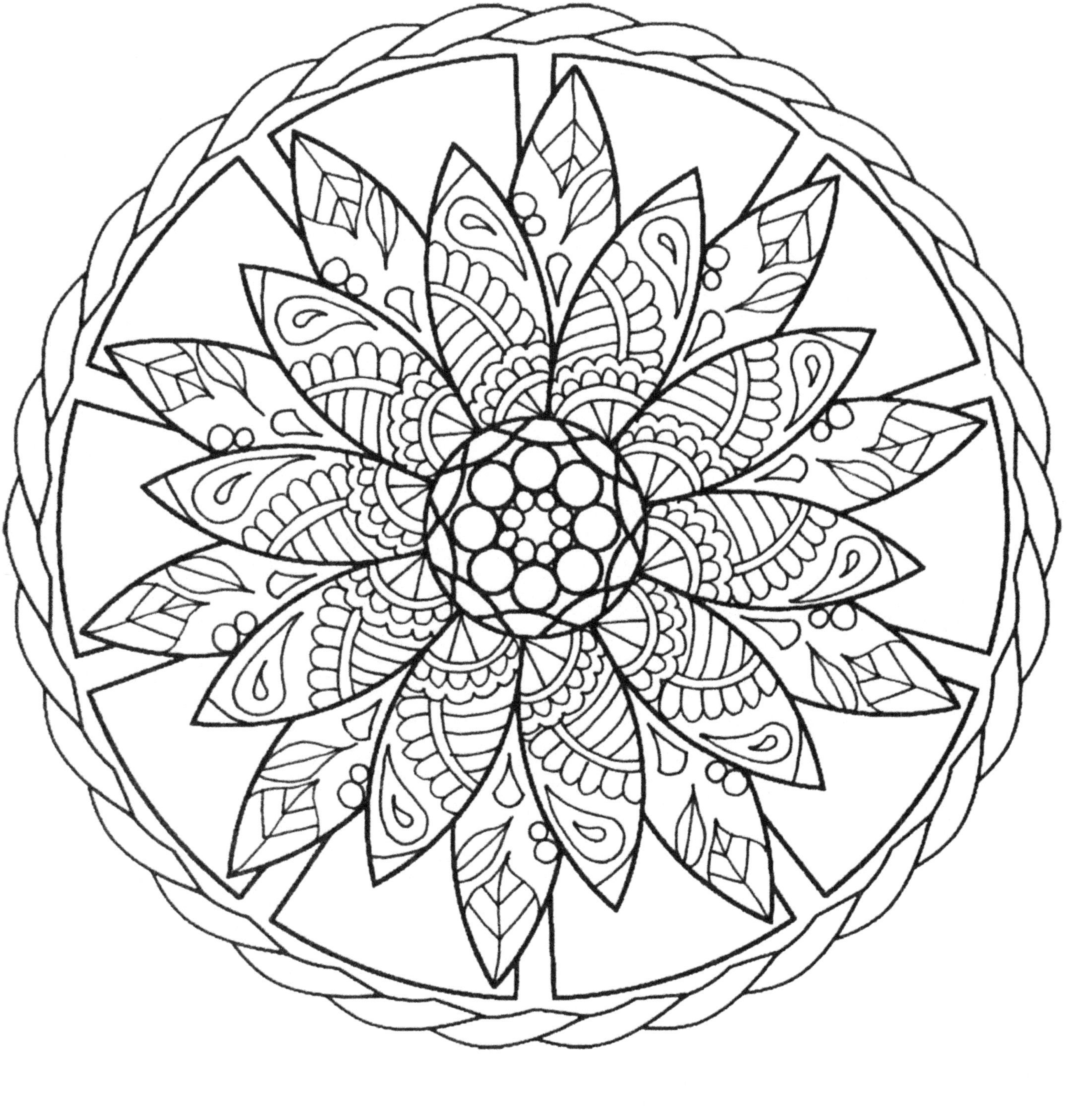

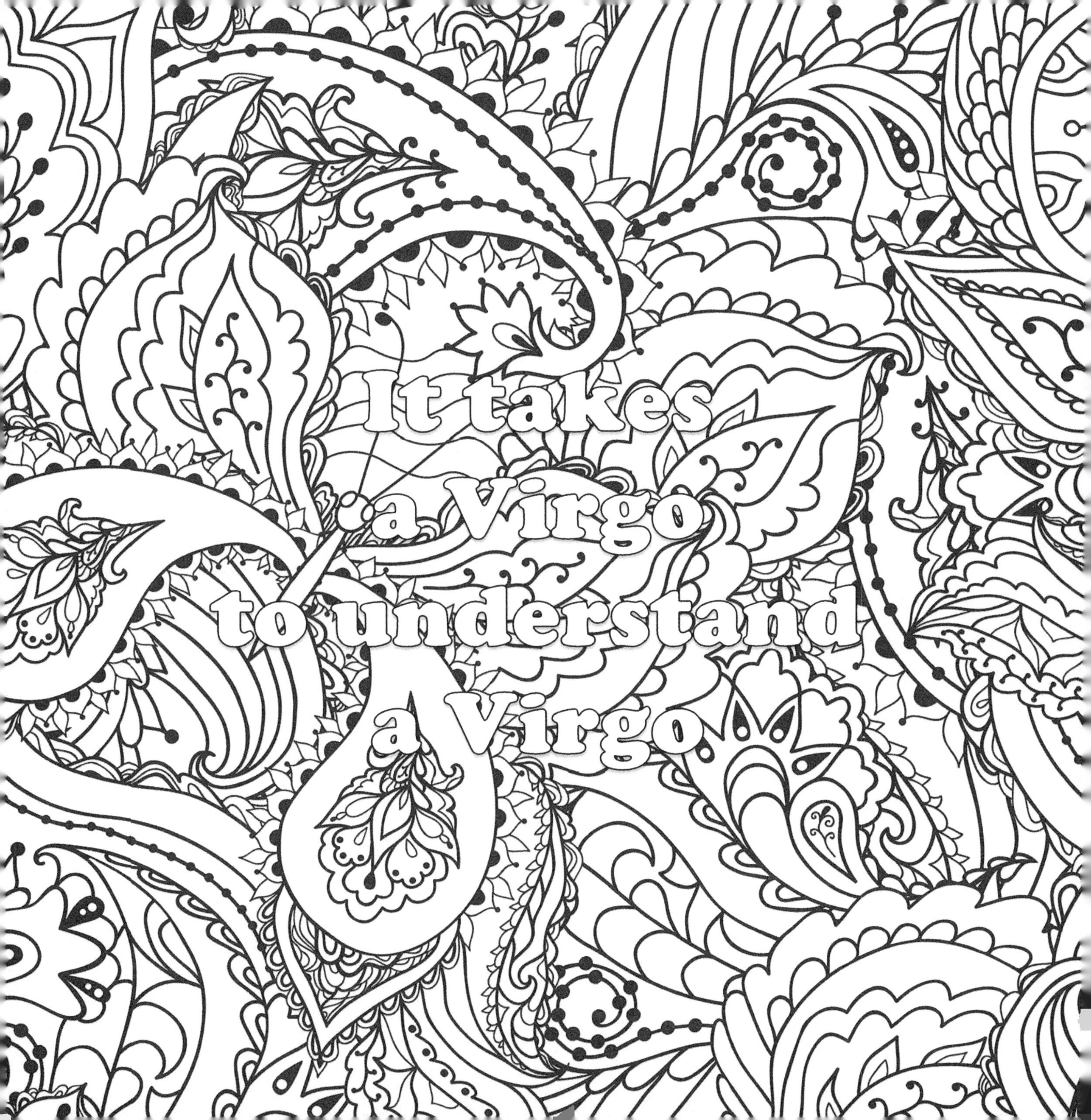
It takes
a Virgo
to understand
a Virgo

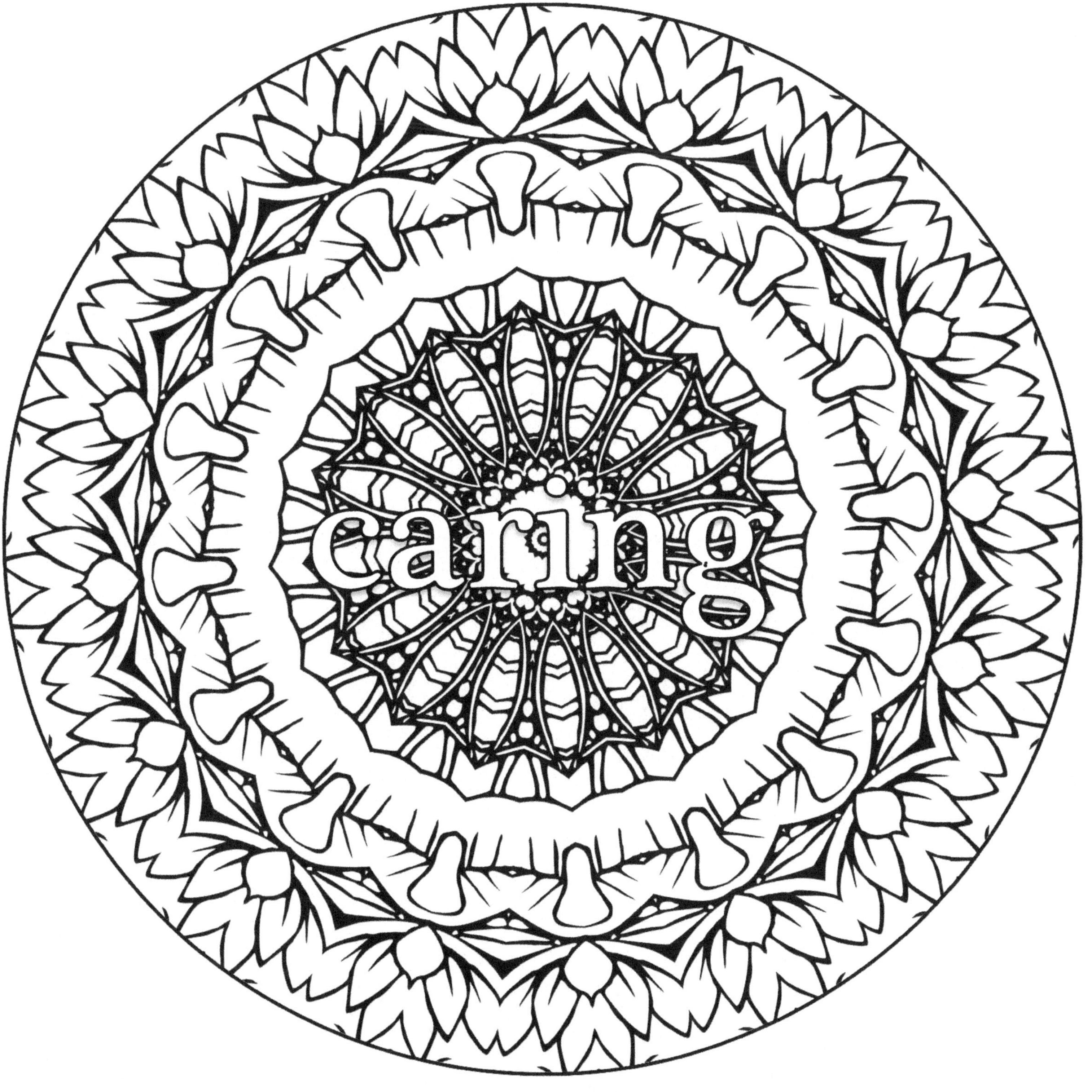
caring

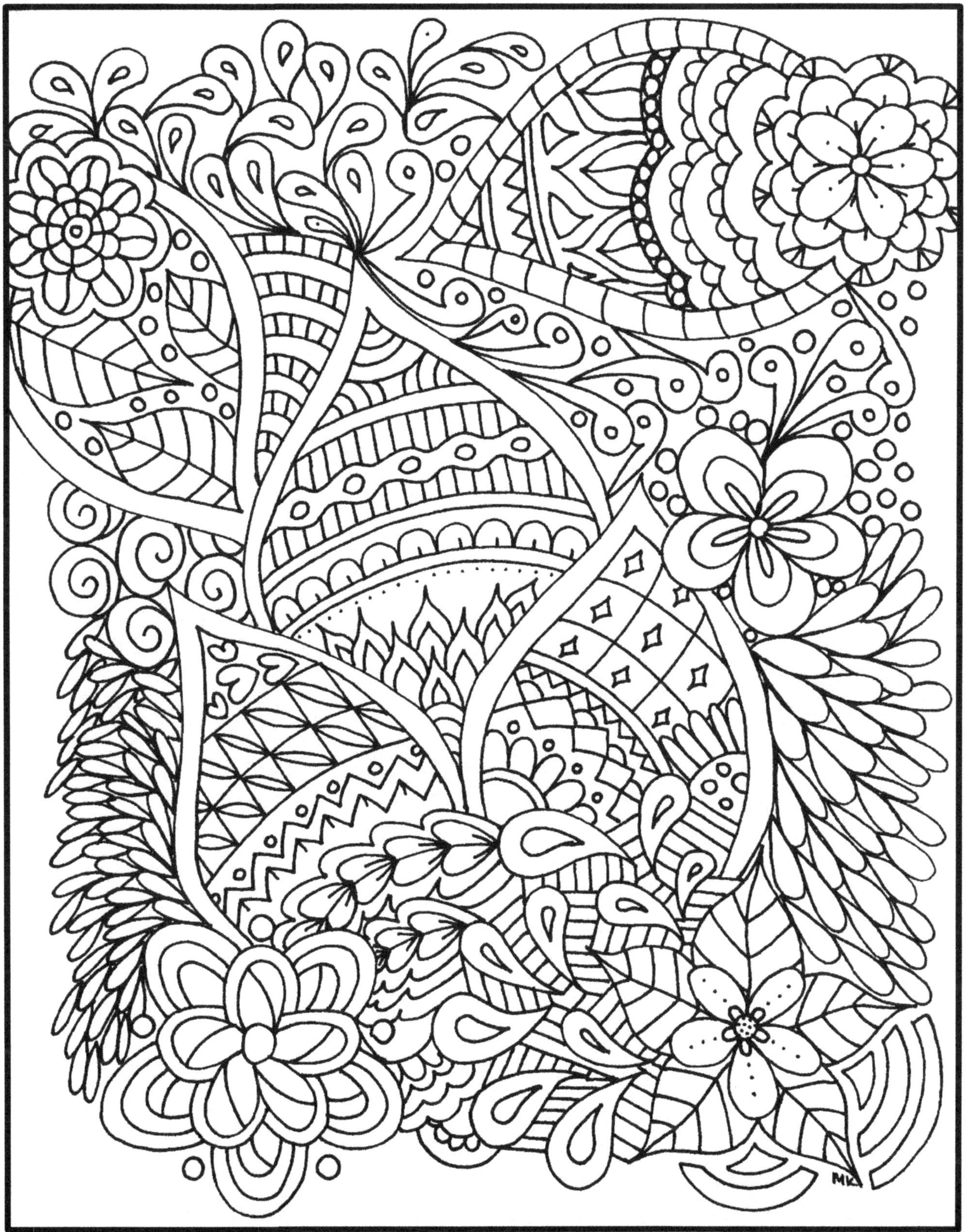
MK

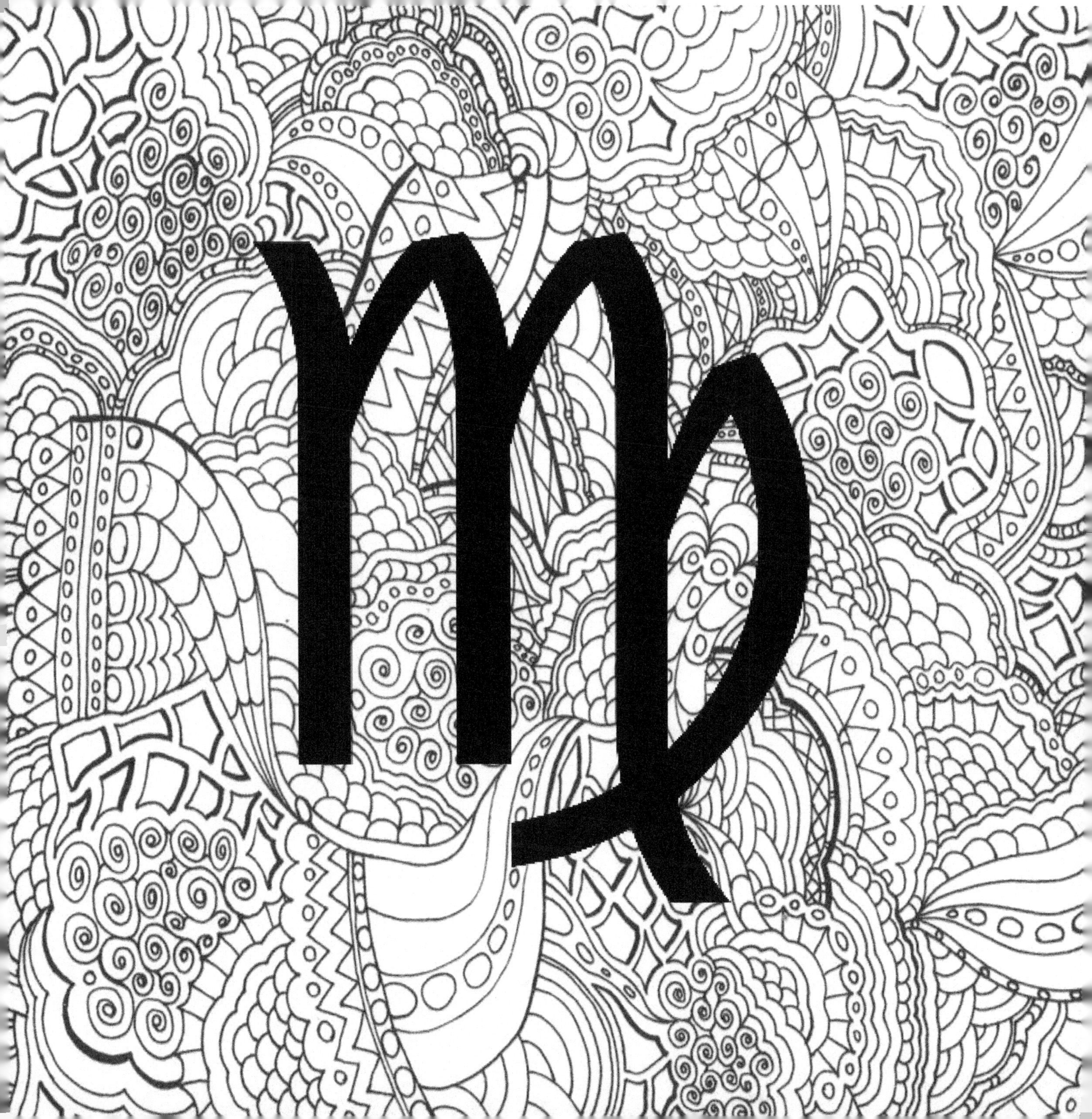

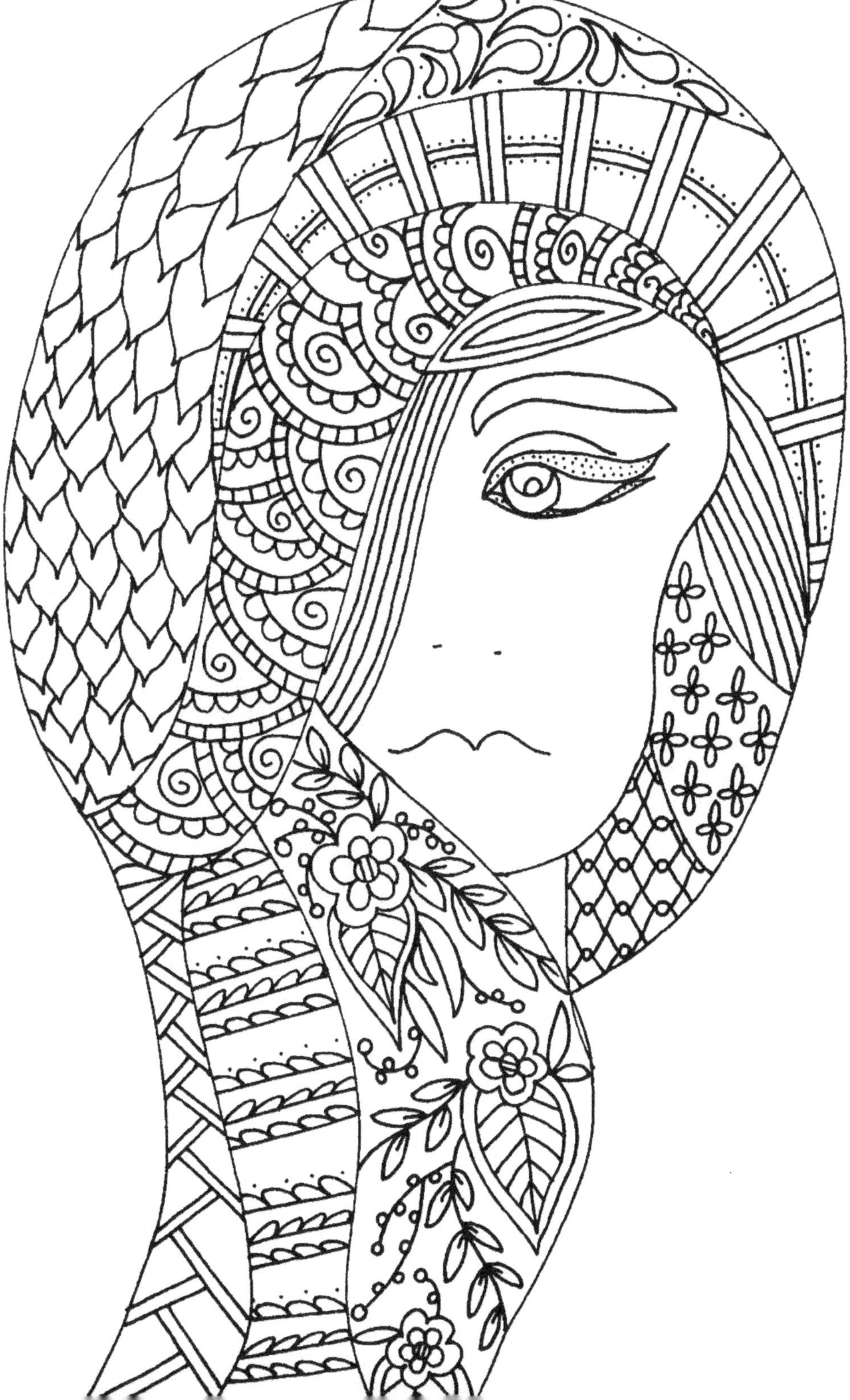

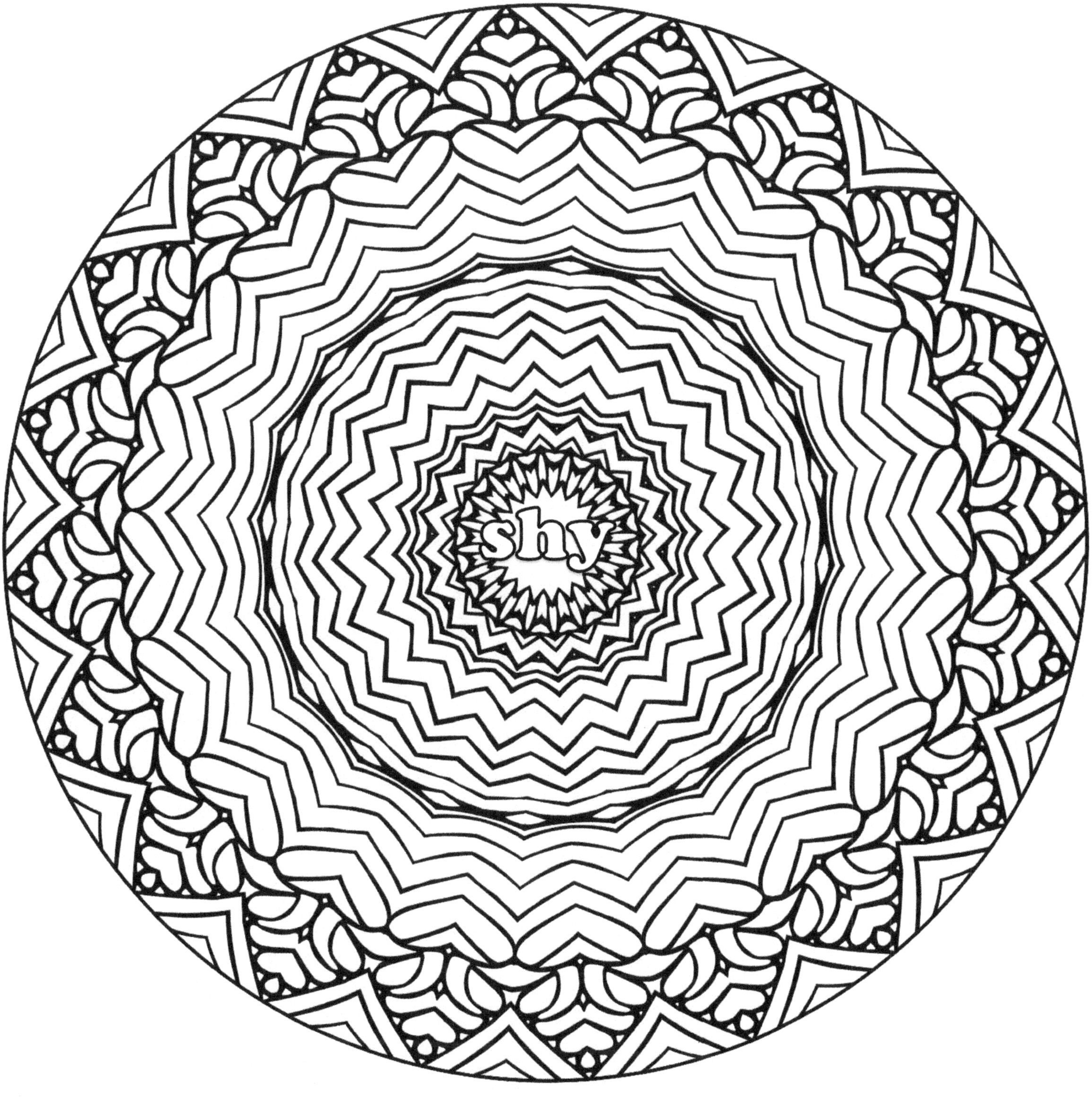
shy

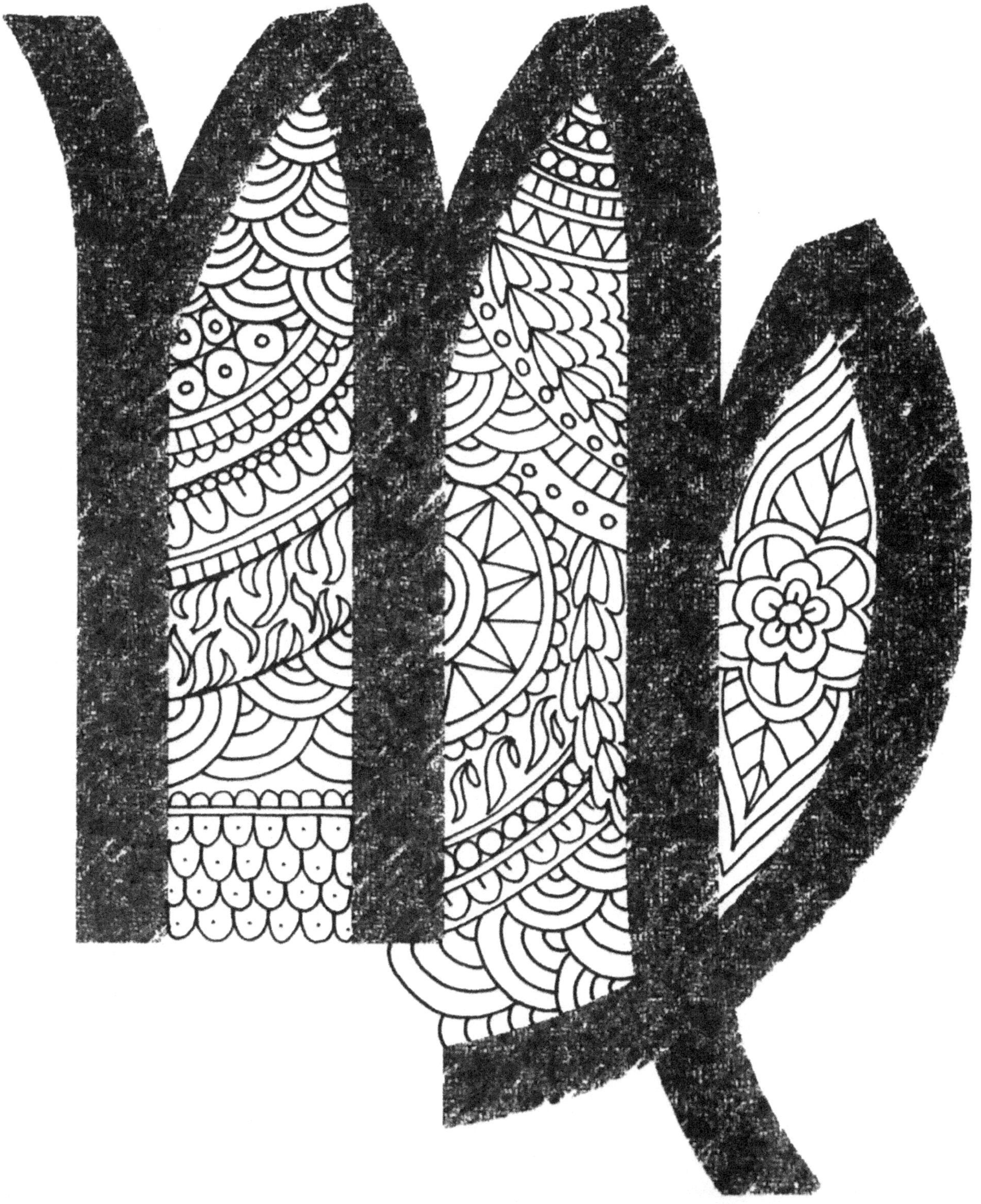

modest
patient
judicious
reserved

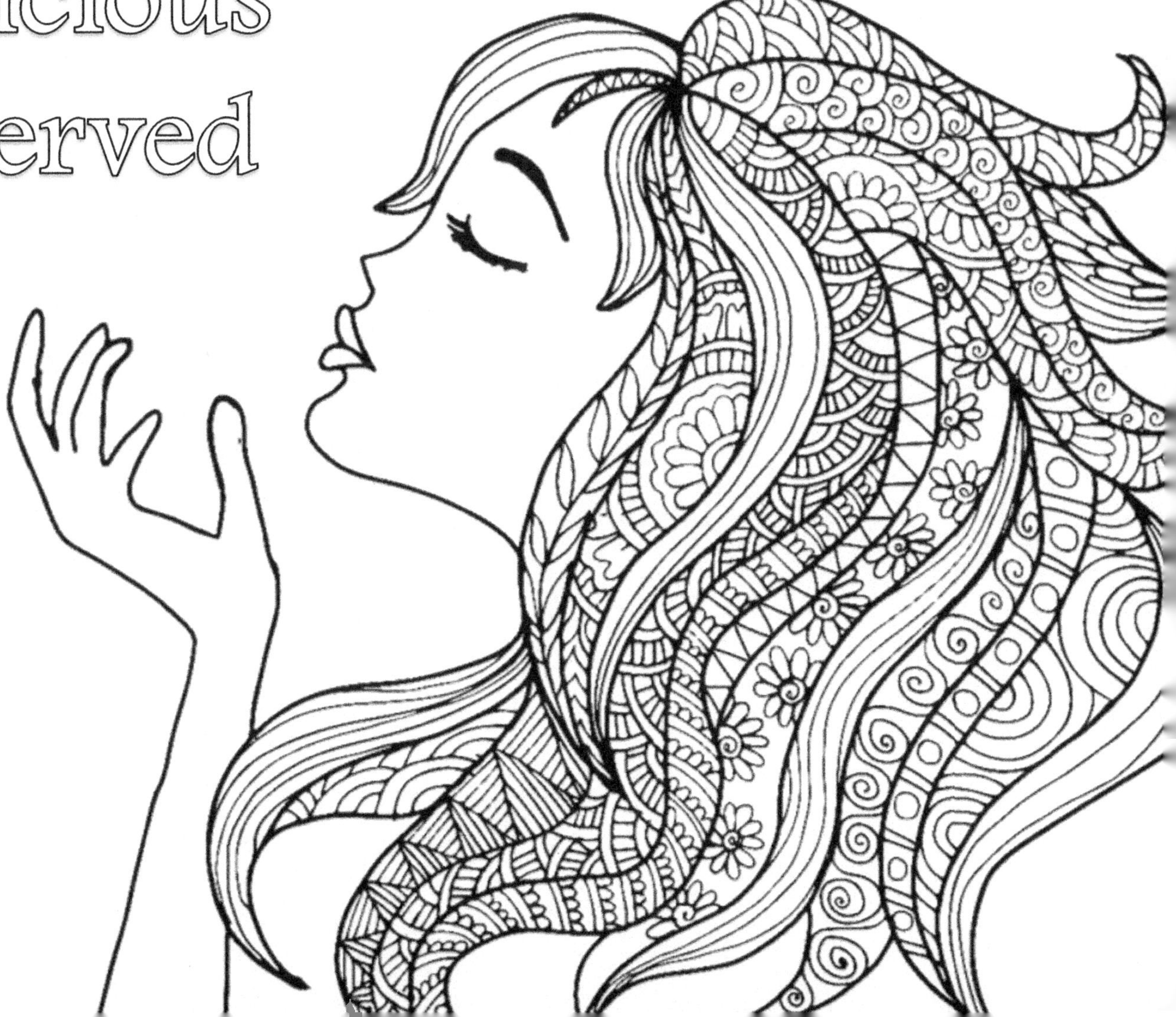

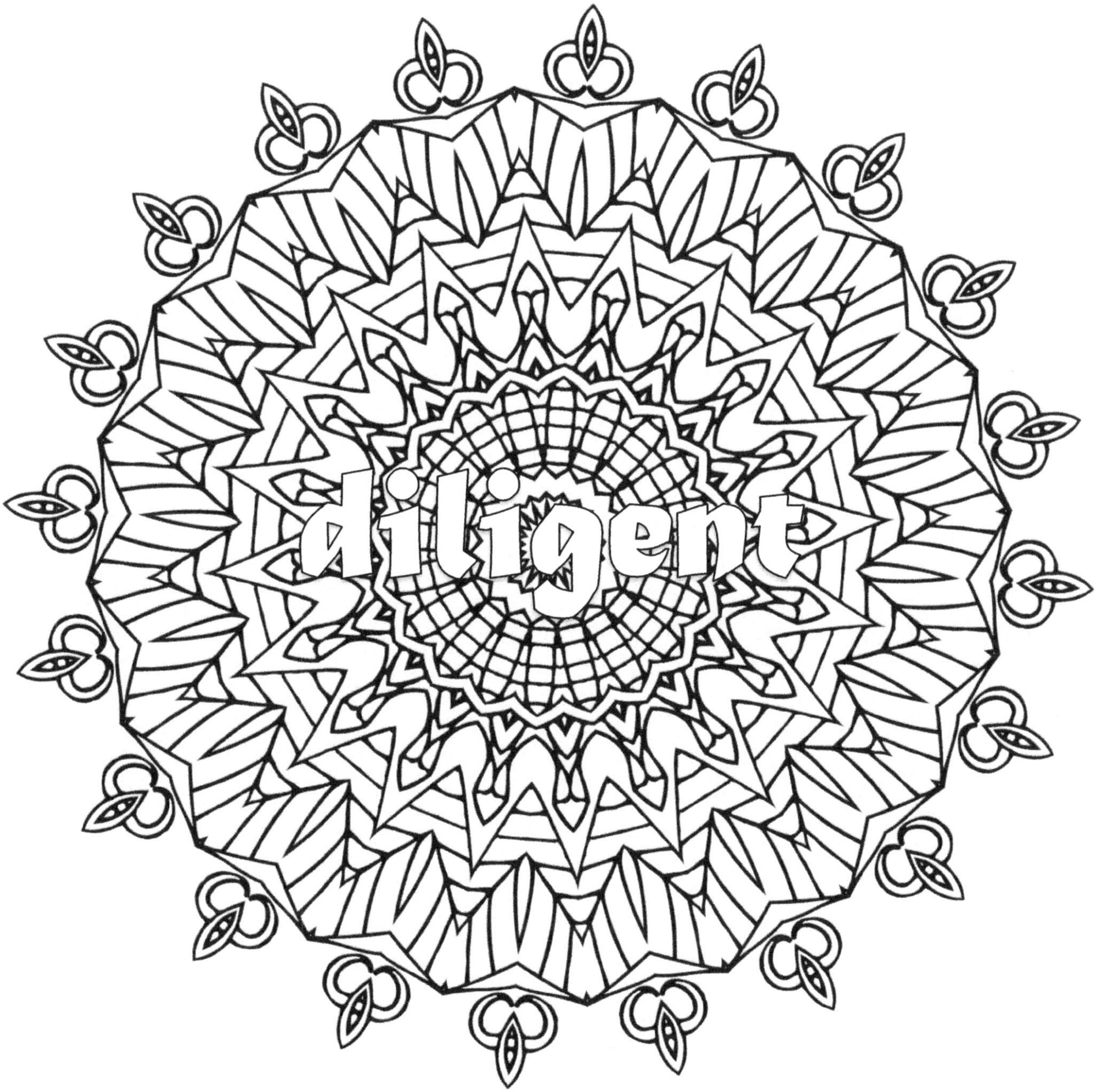
diligent

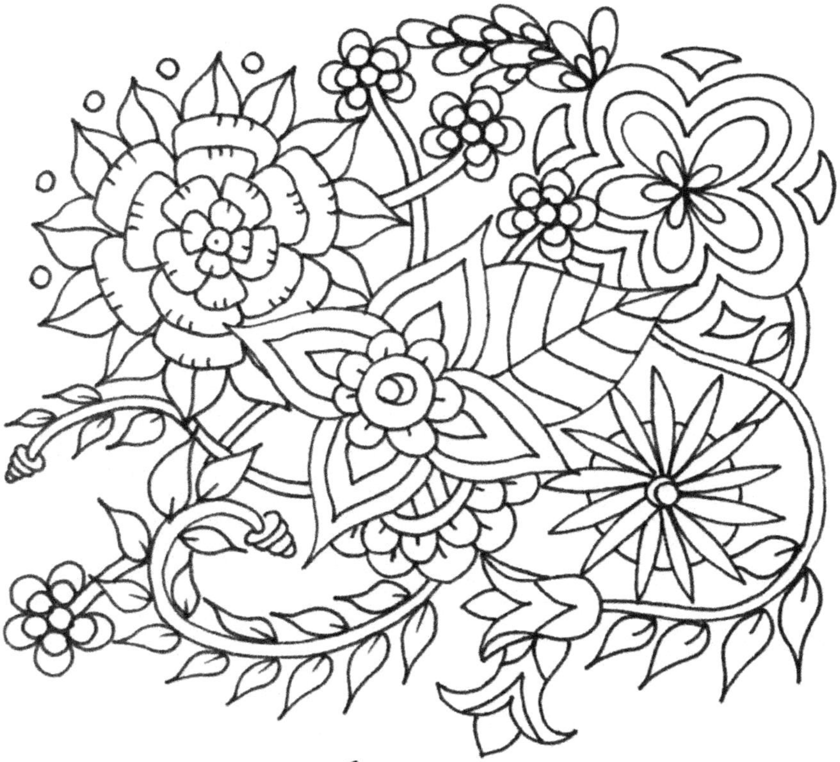

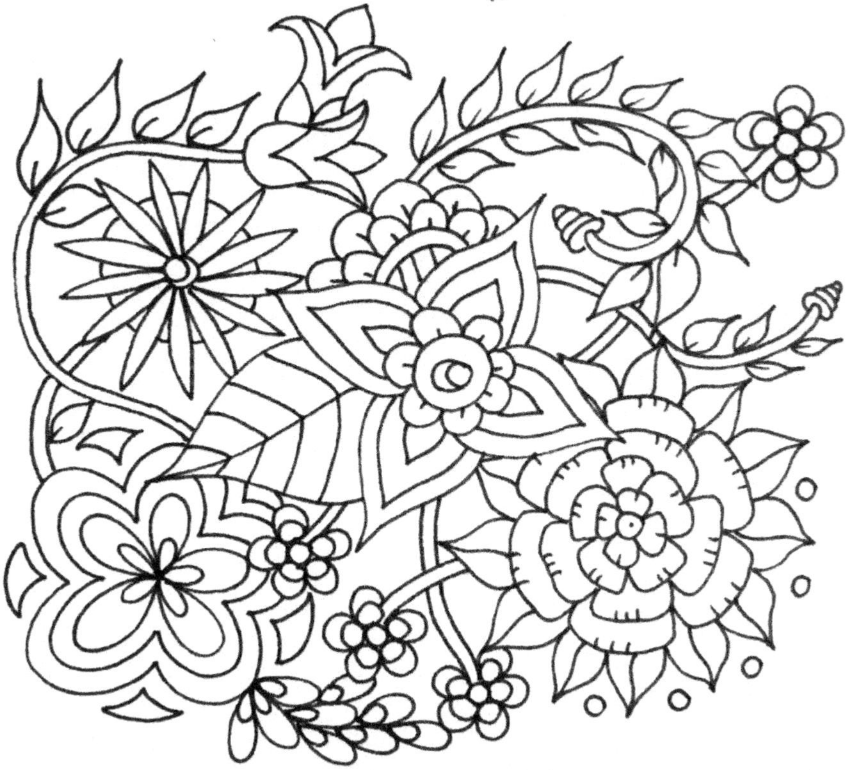

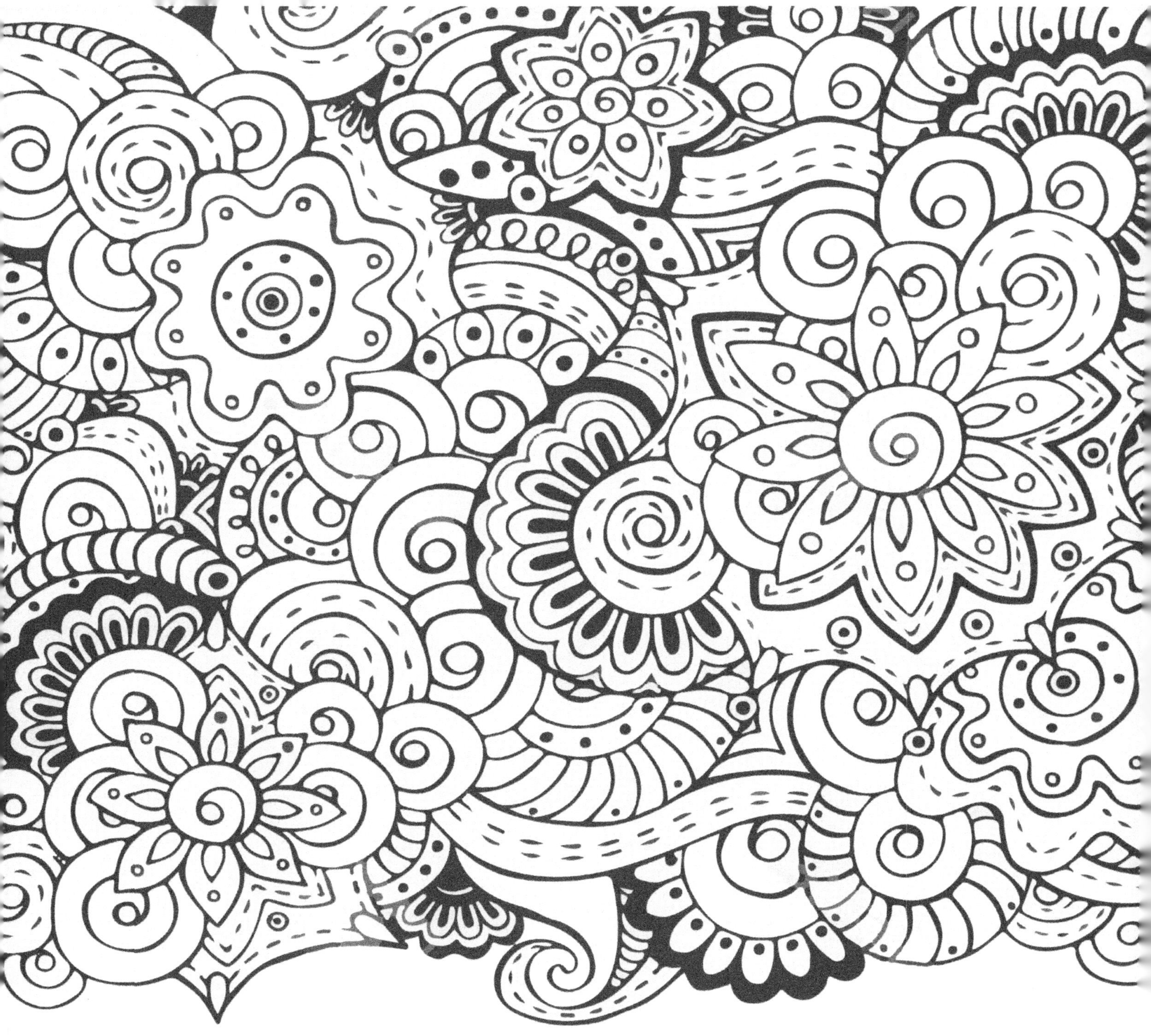

Virgos love the company of animals and nature.

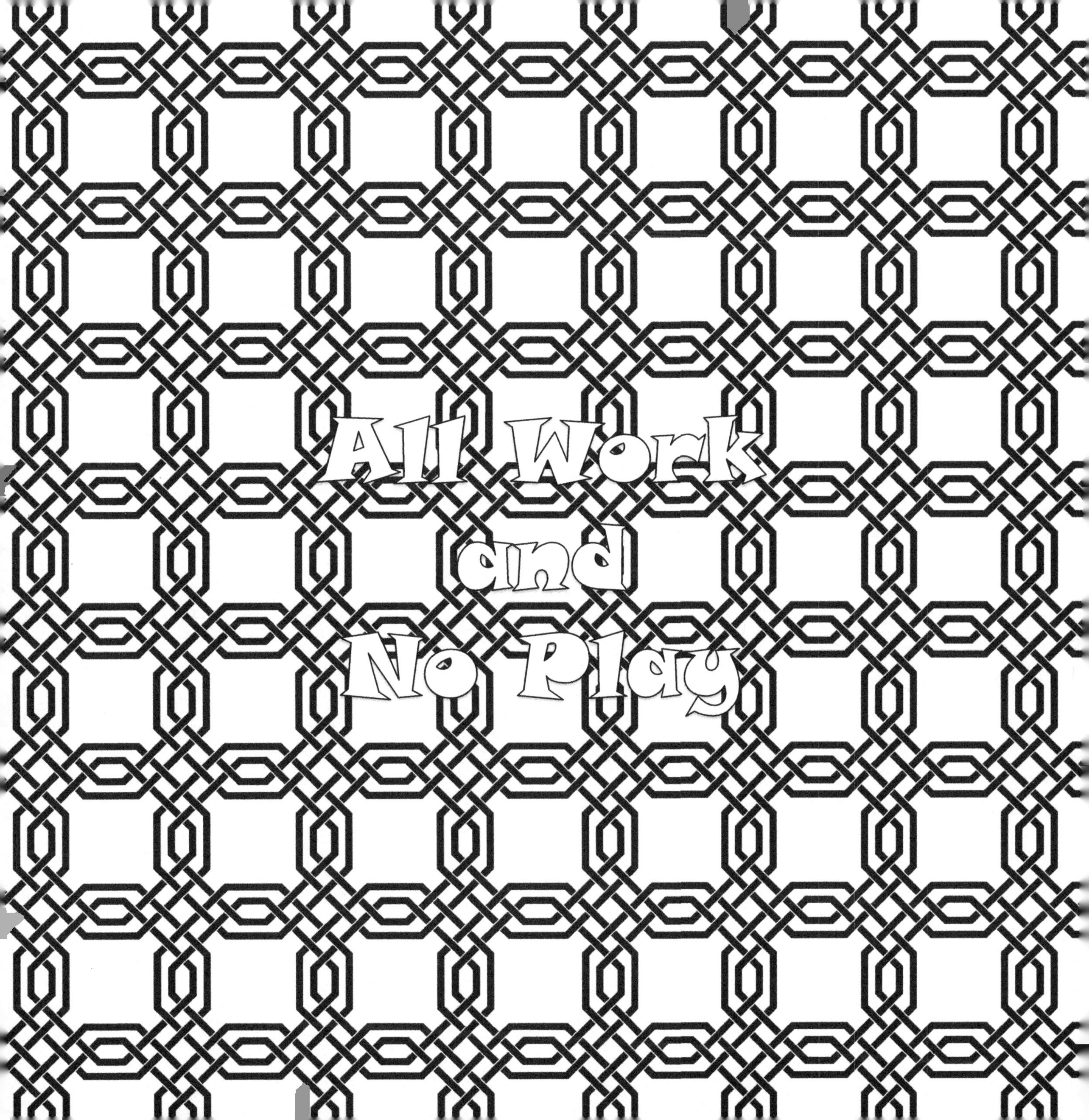
All Work
and
No Play

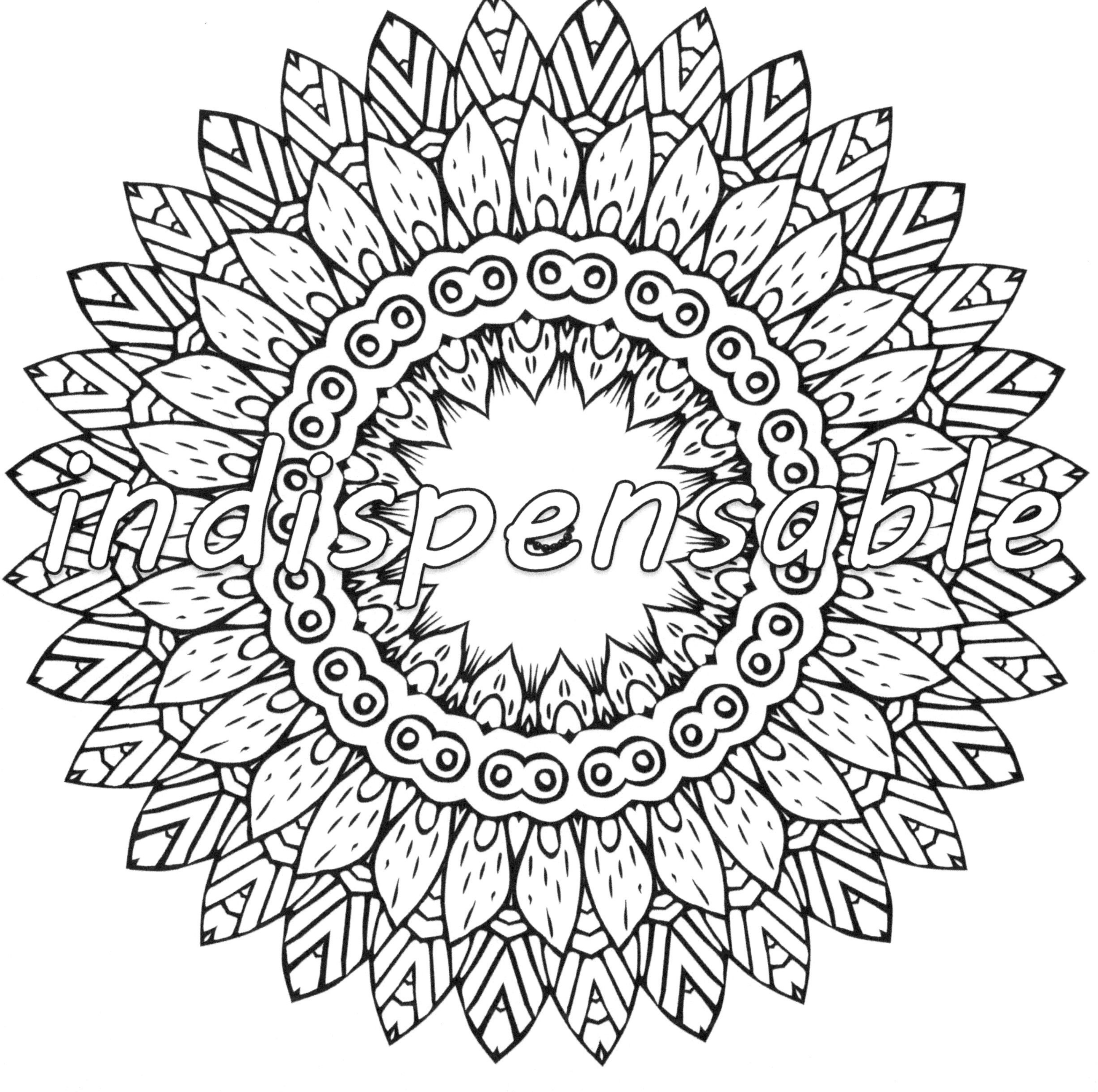
indispensable

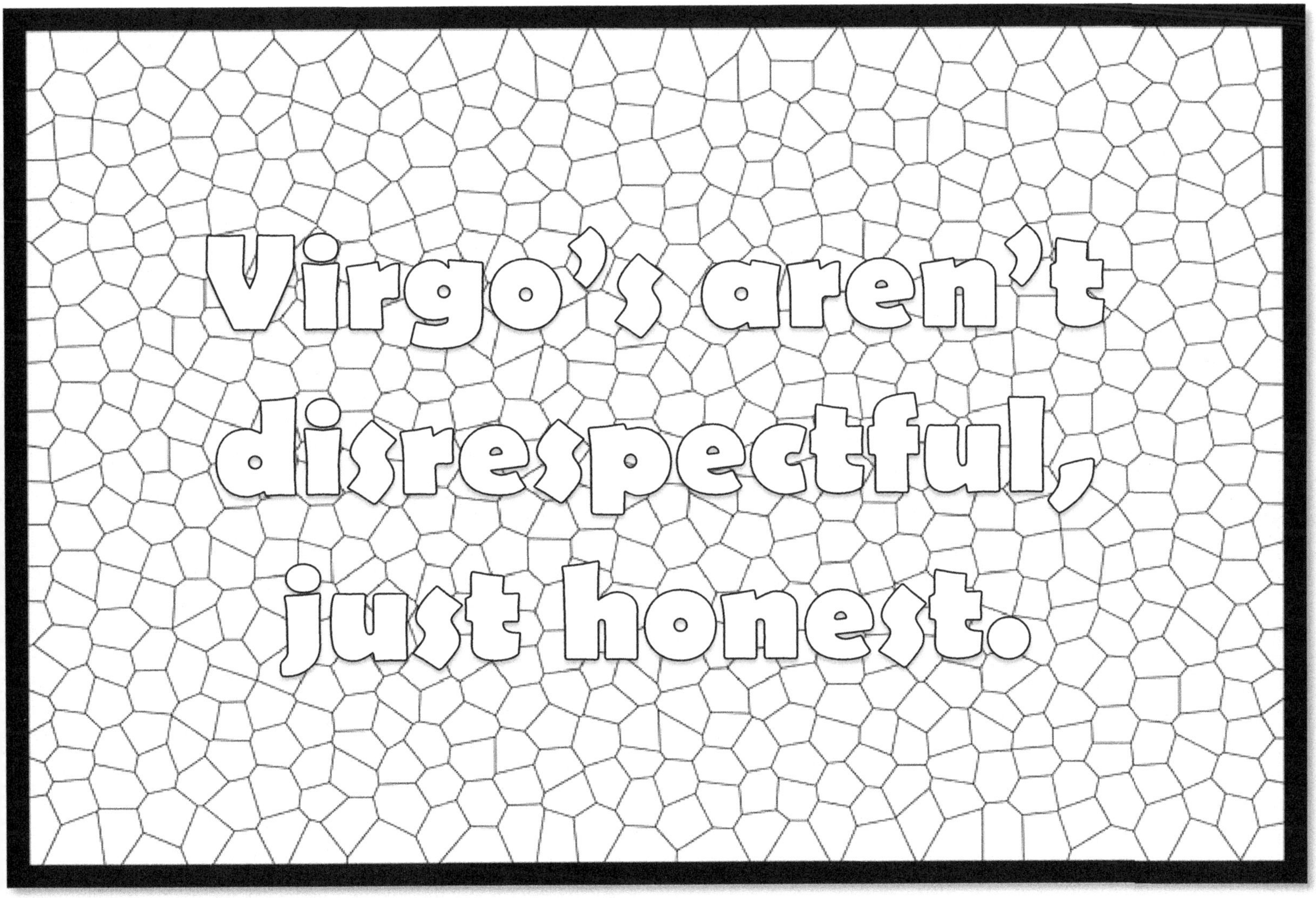
Virgo's aren't
disrespectful,
just honest.

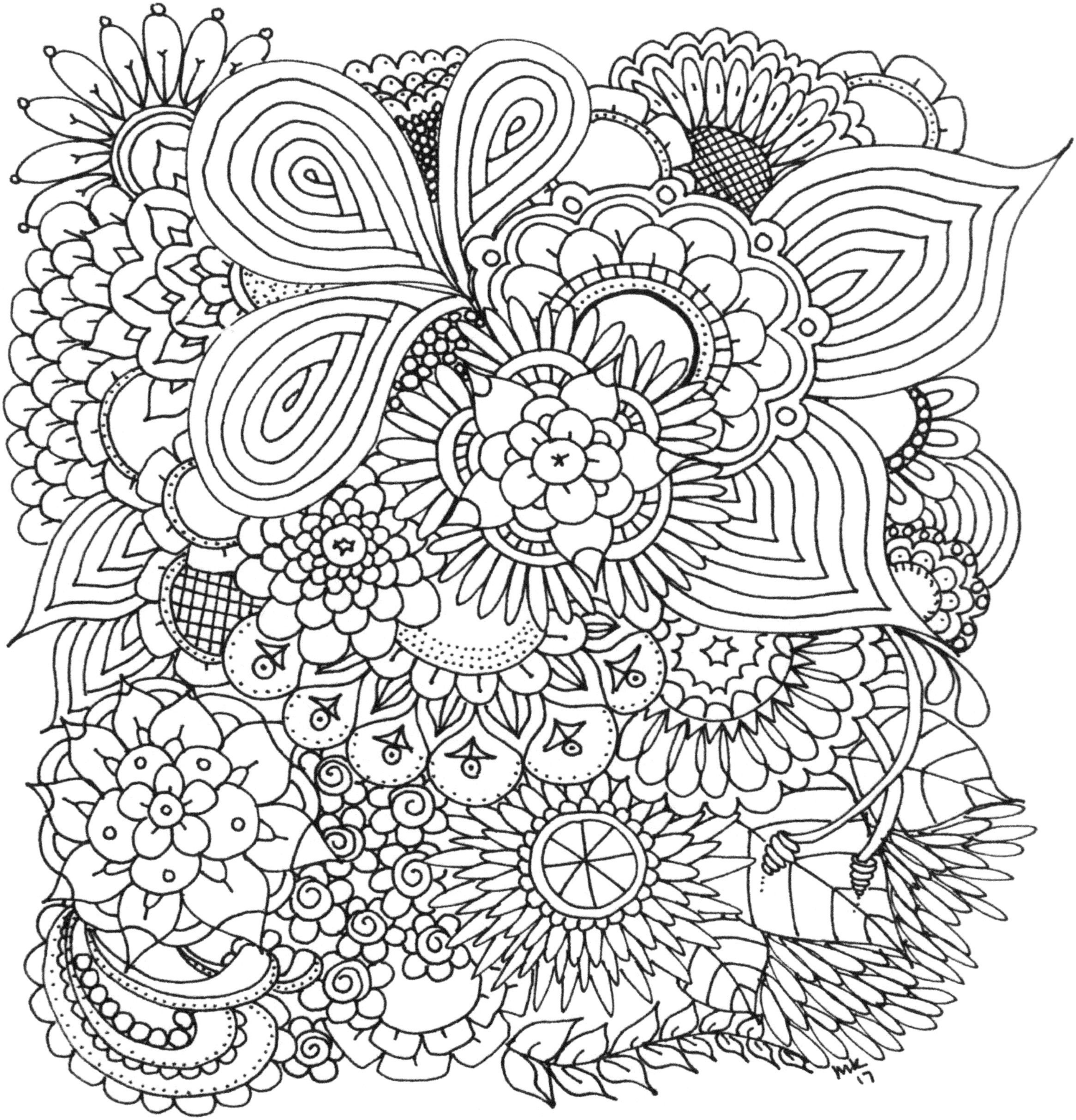

67490077R00046

Made in the USA
Middletown, DE
11 September 2019